Aral
Sea

Jaxartes (Syr Darya)

Oxus (Amu Darya)

Caspian Sea

Alexandria
Eschate

Araxes

Ai Khanoum

BACTRIA   Bactra

HYRKANIA

EDIA

Ecbatana

PARTHIA

ARACHOSIA

ALA
on the Tigris

DRANGIANA

Tigris
Eulaeus   Susa

SUSANIA

ONIA

FAILAKA

Indus

Persepolis

Arab Persian Gulf

MAURYAN
KINGDOM

GEDROSIA

Indian Ocean

NICATOR
SELEUCUS I
AND HIS EMPIRE

NICATOR

SELEUCUS I
AND HIS EMPIRE

LISE HANNESTAD

 Aarhus University Press

Nicator – Seleucus I and his Empire
© The author and Aarhus University Press 2020
Graphic design and cover: Finn Petersen
Type: Electra LT Std. and LinotypeSyntax
Paper: 130g Arctic Volume White
Printed by Narayana Press, Gylling
Printed in Denmark 2020
ISBN 978 87 7219 173 7

Aarhus University Press
Finlandsgade 29
DK-8200 Aarhus N
www.unipress.dk

Published with support from:
Aarhus University Research Foundation
Landsdommer V. Gieses Legat
VELUX Foundation

International distributors:
Oxbow Books Ltd., oxbowbooks.com
ISD, isdistribution.com

PEER
REVIEWED

MIX
Paper from
responsible sources
FSC® C010651

Contents

Introduction

This book is the result of many years of development. In the early 1990s I began working on a book with the preliminary title of *Archaeology of the Seleukid Empire*. Much of the manuscript was written when, due to other pressing tasks, I had to put the project on hold. Some years later, my interest in the Hellenistic Near East was reignited and I found myself with the time to return to the idea of producing a book on the subject. However, my interest had changed from a general interest in the material culture of the Seleucid Empire to something more specific, i.e. a biography of Seleucus I and his empire. This, of course, meant that the source material with which I had to work also changed. It expanded to include a greater focus on the written sources, both literary and epigraphical, in the Greek, Latin and Babylonian cuneiform scripts. But the material culture still plays a substantial role in this study, due to its value for understanding the much discussed issues of continuity and change during the transition from the Achaemenid to the Seleucid Empire, the colonisation scheme of Seleucus and the interaction between local populations and Greek and Macedonian immigrants.

During my years as a young student of classical archaeology in the 1960s, no other scholarly work caught my interest and opened my eyes to the same extent as M. Rostovtzeff's *The Social and Economic History of the Hellenistic World* (1941). The breadth of Rostovtzeff's knowledge and his eminent ability to combine history and archaeology fascinated me completely, and rereading this work over the decades since has only kept my admiration intact. Years later, the pioneering work of S. Sherwin-White and A. Kuhrt, *From Samarkhand to Sardis: A New Approach to the Seleucid Empire* (1993), also made extensive use of both written sources and archaeological material. By that time, I had myself been working with Hellenistic material from the Near East over a long period, and, though I do not agree with the main thesis of the book, i.e. that the Seleucid kingdom was simply a successor of the Achaemenid Empire, it definitely brought new life to the study of the Hellenistic East.

This is not the first biography on Seleucus. Indeed, within the last 50 years, two such books have appeared: A. Mehl, *Seleukos Nikator und sein Reich* (1970) and J.D. Grainger, *Seleukos Nikator* (1990). So what is it that keeps generation after generation of scholars fascinated by Seleucus? The answer may of course vary from person to person, but perhaps Seleucus' life as a whole is the simple answer. From the outset of the chain of events beginning with Alexander's expedition in 333, Seleucus was an unlikely winner of the bid for power following Alexander's death in 323, and was only appointed satrap under the Triparadeisus agreement three years later. Until the culmination of the Babylonian War (see chapter 4) he was not in the same league as Antigonus, Ptolemy or Lysimachus. However, by the end, he was not only the last surviving Diadoch, but he was also undefeated in the great battles between the Diadochs which characterised the period. Later, this led to him being given the surname Nicator.[1] In 301 he contributed decisively to the defeat of Antigonus at Ipsus and in 281 he defeated Lysimachus at Corupedium. By this time, the two combatants were both in their late 70s and had spent most of their adult lives campaigning. Following this last battle, Seleucus wanted to move on to his old homeland, Macedonia, but was murdered shortly after reaching the European mainland (see chapter 5). Thus ended an epoch that had begun with Alexander's anabasis more than 50 years earlier.

Written sources

The literary sources on Seleucus' life are few; in fact, he is the least mentioned of the Diadochs in the preserved Greek and Roman literature. Unlike Ptolemy, he did not himself, as far as we know, leave memoirs or any other written evidence. He seems to have had no Greek historian at his court, as Eumenes and later Antigonus had Hieronymus of Cardia; if he did, no evidence is preserved, apart, perhaps, from a number of myths about Seleucus whose origins are lost in the mists of time. It is possible that Appian used such a source (see below).

Much of the preserved Greco-Roman historical material on the early Hellenistic period is secondary, based on works of earlier Greek authors. This is also the case for the time of Alexander and his Successors. Our

---

[1]   For example, an inscription in Magnesia from the time of Antiochus III (OGIS 233; see also chapter 8).

best source for the latter is Arrian's *Alexander's Anabasis*.[2] Arrian explicitly states that he has based his work on those of two contemporary eyewitness sources: on the 'memories' of Ptolemy and Aristobulus, who was probably an engineer or architect. He also notes when he has used the official Royal Diaries, the so-called *Ephemerides*.[3] In his preface, Arrian presents the following argument:

'Wherever Ptolemy son of Lagus and Aristobulus son of Aristobulus have both given the same accounts of Alexander son of Philip, it is my practice to record what they say as completely true, but where they differ, to select the version I regard as more trustworthy and also better worth telling. In fact other writers have given a variety of accounts of Alexander, nor is there any other figure of whom there are more historians who are more contradictory of each other, but in my view Ptolemy and Aristobulus are more trustworthy in their narrative, since Aristobulus took part in King Alexander's expedition, and Ptolemy not only did the same, but as he himself was a king, mendacity would have been more dishonourable for him than for anyone else; again both wrote when Alexander was dead and neither was under any constraint or hope of gain to make him set down anything but what actually happened.'[4]

When reading Arrian, one clearly notes a change in the narrative. In the first books on Alexander's three great battles against Darius until he leaves Susa (III.16), the style is rather stiff, with stress on the names of high-ranking officers; for this part, one could imagine that Ptolemy used the Royal Diaries (*Ephemerides*).[5] After the stay in Susa (book III.17 onwards), the narrative becomes much more lively, often with a focus on Ptolemy himself. It is quite possible that from this point onwards Ptolemy often relied on his own diaries. Arrian also wrote a work titled *Events after Alexander*. Hieronymus was probably the main source for this,[6] but, sadly, only fragments are preserved.

The main literary source for the period after the death of Alexander is Diodorus Siculus, who wrote a *Bibliotheca Historica* in 40 volumes between 60 and 30 BC; books I–V and XI–XX survive. Books XVIII–XX

---

2   For Arrian and his work, see Cartledge, P. in Romm and Mensch, XIII–XXVIII (2012); also Baynham, E.
    ibid. 325–32; Bosworth 1988.
3   For a discussion of their origin, see Bosworth 1988, 157–84.
4   Translation P.A. Brunt, Loeb 1976.
5   Also, Hammond is of the opinion that Alexander's Diaries were accessible to Ptolemy, probably being
    kept in Alexandria (1988, 17).
6   Walbank 1988, 96.

and the preserved fragments of book XXI[7] treat the time of the Diadochs. These books clearly form a unified section that differs from the preceding book XVII.[8] For this period, Diodorus' main source was undoubtedly Hieronymus of Cardia, who held high posts under Eumenes, Antigonus and Demetrius and his son Antigonus Gonatas, and wrote a *History of the Successors* (see Diod. Sic. XVIII. 42.1), of which only a few fragments are preserved. In Antiquity his style was considered tedious and unreadable in large parts (Dionysius Hal. *Comp.* 4.3 = *FGrH* 154 T12).

Diodorus' value as a source has often been questioned by modern historians, and, in contrast to Arrian, he makes no references to his sources. However, one should not underestimate the enormous value that his work presents, being the only preserved nearly complete and detailed work on the period of the Diadochs. His work is structured so as to present separately events in Asia and Europe (divided into Greek and Roman parts) for each year – more or less.[9] His main source for Asia seems to have been Hieronymus of Cardia, a contemporary of the Diadochs who wrote a history of the period 323–272. He first served Eumenes, then Antigonus, Demetrius and at the end Antigonus Gonatanas.

Plutarch, in his *Parallel Lives* written around and after AD 100 (Plutarch died in AD 120), undoubtedly also draws on Hieronymus in his *Lives of Eumenes and Demetrius*. However, due to the subject, it informs us of Seleucus only in relation to Demetrius' life.

Our sources for the last period of Seleucus' life are scanty. The loss of most of Diodorus' book XXI is particularly frustrating, since, in this book, Seleucus, who at this point in the narrative had direct connections with political development close to the Mediterranean and went on to become a principal character on the political scene over the course of the next two decades, must have been much more visible than in preceding sections.

Another comprehensive work on Alexander and the period of the Diadochs was the *Historiae Philippicae* of Pompeius Trogus (a historian of the Augustan period). However, this is known only from excerpts adopted by a number of Christian authors and an epitome by Justin. In book XV there is a longer passage on Seleucus, mainly concerning the myths that came to be told about him (see chapter 7) and his campaign to India; books XVI–XVII, which cover the whole period, form the only continuous narrative from Ipsus to the death of Seleucus.

---

7 Diodorus' books XXI–XL are only preserved in fragments in Photius and Byzantine excerpts.
8 See Hornblower 1981, 32–9.
9 For a discussion of the sources for the Diadoch period, see, e.g., Billows 1990, Appendix 1.

Of particular importance for the last phase of Seleucus' life is Memnon's history of Heraclea Pontica, his native city. This work, probably written in the first century AD, is preserved only in an epitome of Photius. Memnon seems to have used as his source the historian Nymphis, who in the middle of the third century wrote a work called *Concerning Alexander and his Descendants*, together with two other works, all preserved in fragments only. Memnon's work offers, in particular, information on the very last period of Seleucus' life, on Lysimachus' death, on the months after the battle at Corupedium and on the murder of Seleucus by Ptolemy Keraunus.

Appian's *Syrian Wars*, part of his *Roman History* written in the middle of the second century AD, is the source that focuses most directly on the life of Seleucus, in a digression on how the Macedonians had conquered Syria (App. *Syr.* 52–61). Appian's history is a mix of a short presentation on political history and what he calls prophecies. He stresses Seleucus' achievements as city founder, something about which the other sources tell us very little. He also relates in detail the story of Antiochus falling in love with Stratonice and how this developed. Clearly, Appian took much of this from one or more sources that may have been written at the Seleucid court.

The Greek historian Polybius wrote his *Histories*, covering the period 264–146, as a contemporary eyewitness to a significant part of the period. In his narrative of the fifth Syrian war between Antiochus III and Ptolemy V of Egypt, he includes (V.67) the convention between Seleucus, Lysimachus and Cassander after Ipsus (see chapter 5).

Pausanias, the indefatigable traveller, who wrote his *Description of Greece* in the second century AD, is little appreciated by historians but of great interest to archaeologists. Characteristic of his descriptions of sites in Greece are long passages telling of myths or historical figures or events. Thus, in his description of the Agora in Athens he details a number of bronze statues in front of the stoa poikile, including one of Solon 'and, a little farther away' one of Seleucus, whose future prosperity was 'foreshadowed by unmistakable signs'. Pausanias continues with a narrative of Seleucus' life, covering in particular the last months of his life and his death.

A source that is unfortunately preserved only in fragments is that written by the Babylonian priest Berossus, who composed a history of Babylonia in Greek dedicated to Antiochus I (*FGrH* 680 T2). None of the preserved fragments concerns the Hellenistic period.

As to Greek epigraphical sources, very few from Seleucus' time are preserved, and, for this reason, I have included in this book a number from the times of Antigonus and Antiochus (in particular in chapter 6 on administration). The majority are from Asia Minor.

Of the Babylonian sources,[10] the most important are the *Babylonian Chronicles of the Hellenistic period*.[11] These take the form of cuneiform tablets written during the Seleucid period by Babylonian scribes of the Esagil temple in Babylon, probably using the historical information sometimes included in the *Astronomical Diaries* (see below) as their principal source. The main text concerning the time of Seleucus is written on one tablet, now broken into two pieces (ABC 10/BCHP 3),[12] which offers us glimpses of the period when Seleucus became satrap of Babylonia and is particularly important regarding the so-called Babylonian War, which is not even mentioned by Diodorus. The tablet has also reopened the question of chronology from the time of the agreement of Triparadeisus until the end of Antigonus' war with Eumenes. Another tablet, BCHP 9, concerns the last months of the king's life.[13]

The *Astronomical Diaries* has been edited by Sachs and Hunger. Particularly relevant is their Vol I, covering the period 652–262. Apart from astronomical information, the *Diaries* also report on prices of commodities, river levels and historical events. The *Babylonian King Lists* are lists of kings and the lengths of their reigns, one from Babylon and one from Uruk.[14]

The material sources

The quantity of archaeological evidence from the time of Seleucus and his son Antiochus has grown significantly in recent years due to a number of important excavations. In chapter 8, on Seleucus as coloniser, I focus on a number of sites in order to present cities that were probably founded by him or his son, with the following question in mind: was there a specific layout characteristic of these cities? Chapter 9 deals with the material culture of different parts of the kingdom. It is important, of course, to realise

---

10   For cuneiform documentation on the history of the Diadoch period, see Boiy 2013.
11   For an introduction to the *Babylonian Chronicles*, see Waerzegger 2012.
12   The tablet is about 17 cm long and 6–6.5 cm wide. It probably had four columns of text: two on the obverse and two on the reverse, of which column 2 on the obverse and column 1 on the reverse are lost. ABC stands for the edition of Grayson; BCHP for the online edition of Finkel and van der Spek.
13   Two non-joining fragments of a tablet. For both tablets I have used Finkel's and van der Spek's online presentation and translations https://www.livius.org/sources/about/mesopotamian-chronicles/ In the most recent online update it is announced that the book Finkel, I.L and R.J. van der Spek and R. Pirngruber. *Babylonian Chronographic Texts from the Hellenistic Period* will appear in 2020.
14   See Boiy 2011.

that the dating of material culture can rarely be as precise as that of political history. In this chapter, I have, therefore, taken a broader view, though I attempt, as far as possible, to concentrate on the time of Seleucus and Antiochus or sometimes the early Seleucid period. The aim here is to study the cultural meeting of Greek and local cultures.

Numismatics

Numismatics is usually considered a separate discipline from archaeology, and offers much more precise dating possibilities. The study of coins offers rich information regarding both economic and ideological issues, and is, therefore, adopted mainly in chapters 6–7, but also in chapter 8 when attempting to date the foundations of the colonies.

Chronology

In this book, the so-called low chronology first proposed by B.E. Manni (1949) has been used for the period from the meeting at Triparadeisus to Antigonus' campaign in Syria and Phoenicia. For various opinions regarding the chronology of this period, see Boiy 2007. T. Boiy prefers the low chronology for Perdiccas' death and the meeting at Triparadeisus,[15] but the high chronology for the Babylonian War (2007, table 25). See chapter 3 for my scepticism as to this change of chronology.

Acknowledgements

Several colleagues and friends have supported my work throughout. In particular I want to thank Toennes Bekker-Nielsen for having read and given many useful suggestions to one of the chapters; to Vinnie Nørskov and Niels, my husband, for assistance with the illustrations; and to Else Roesdahl, Flemming Hoejlund and Steffen Terp Laursen for many interesting discussions. Thanks also go to my patient and always optimistic editor Sanne Lind Hansen.

Last but not least I wish to thank Aarhus University Research Foundation, Landsdommer V. Gieses Legat, and the Velux Foundation warmly for their financial support.

---

15   See also Anson 2002/2003.

CHAPTER 1

Campaigning
with Alexander

At dawn on a spring day in late April or early May[1] 326 BC, after a night of heavy rain and wind (Arr. *Anab.* V.12.4), Alexander crossed the Hydaspes river in northern India as the bad weather subsided. After weeks of careful preparations – including having the vessels used to cross the Indus brought up and made ready, and having parts of the army move up and down along the river bank to leave the Indian king Porus, who was camped on the opposite bank, in total uncertainty as to what was planned – Alexander decided that the time had come to unleash a surprise attack. Ships and rafts were now ready to take a portion of the army across the river, unseen by Porus' scouts. 'Alexander in person embarked on a triaconter and began the passage and with him Ptolemy,[2] Perdiccas and Lysimachus, bodyguards, and Seleucus, one of the Companions, who afterwards became king, and half the hypaspists'.[3]

No-one present in the boat can have imagined that, just three years later, the men listed here by name were all to play major roles in the power struggle that took place after Alexander's death. Since this is the first time that Seleucus is mentioned by Arrian, the author takes the opportunity to add that he was a Companion who later became king.[4] In the first phase of the battle, in which Alexander fought against the son of Porus, Arrian mentions in his description of the battle order (V.13.4) that 'next to the cavalry he [Alexander] marshalled from the infantry the royal hypaspists under Seleucus, then the royal *agema*, and next the rest of the hypaspists,

---

1   Arr. *Anab.* V.19.3 mentions the month of Mounykhion, which corresponds to late April/early May.
2   According to Quintus Curtius VIII.18–19, Ptolemy was not in the boat, but rather led a diversionary manoeuvre on the riverbank.
3   Translation P.A. Brunt, Loeb 1976. All translations of Arrian are taken from this version.
4   Lysimachus is also mentioned here for the first time in Arrian's *Anabasis*. In contrast, however, Arrian does not tell us anything about Lysimachus' future role as king.

in order determined by the precedence of the commanders for that day; on the wings of the phalanx on either side he stationed the archers, the Agrianians and the javelin-throwers'. This first stage of the fighting turned out to be essentially a cavalry battle.[5] In the second phase – after Alexander had held back his cavalry to wait for the arrival of the infantry and allowed the foot soldiers to recover from their march while they were protected by the encircling cavalry – he regrouped to meet Porus himself. During the ensuing battle, Seleucus reappears in Arrian's account (V.16.3). Alexander reorganised his forces and now 'Seleucus, Antigenes and Tauron were put in command of the infantry phalanx with orders not to take part in the action until they observed the enemy's phalanx of infantry and their cavalry thrown into confusion by his own cavalry force'. At a later stage of the battle, when the mahouts of the Indian war elephants had brought up their animals against the Macedonian cavalry, the Macedonian forces advanced

Fig. 1 | The Hydaspes River (modern-day Jhelum), a tributary of the Indus, running c. 775 km through northern India and eastern Pakistan.

---

5   Arrian (*Anab.* V.14.3–6) informs us of what Aristobulus 'and others' reports about the beginning of the
     battle, but notes that he has decided to follow Ptolemy's account.

to meet the elephants and, hurling javelins at the mahouts and forming a ring round the animals, they shot at them from all sides. Arrian, probably adopting Ptolemy's version of events, states that 'the action was now without parallel in any previous contest, for the beasts charged into the line of infantry, and, whichever way they turned, began to devastate the Macedonian phalanx, dense though it was, while the Indian cavalry, seeing the infantry fully engaged, wheeled again and themselves charged the cavalry.'[6]

Arrian's description of the battle against Porus bears all the freshness of a personal memory of this event, and thus must surely derive from Ptolemy's narrative. The battle gave Alexander's army the frightening experience of fighting against war elephants; Alexander and his successors learnt their lesson: elephants were to become an important element of early Hellenistic warfare.[7] When Alexander left India, 200 elephants were included in the portion of the forces brought back by Hephaistion. Much later, Seleucus himself would also bring back elephants from India (see chapter 4).

By the time of the Battle of the Hydaspes, eight years had passed since Seleucus had set out from Macedonia as a member of Alexander's army. During this time he must have served well, resulting at some point in his appointment as commander of the royal hypaspists. Neither Arrian nor any of the other sources offer information about the earlier career of Seleucus during Alexander's campaign in Asia. Thus, to assume that Seleucus was a member of the hypaspists from the outset of the campaign is no more than hypothetical.[8] Nonetheless, the list of hypaspist actions in Arrian's *Anabasis* affords us a picture of the types of operations of which Seleucus was to become a leader.

The hypaspists

Arrian offers us a good insight into the purpose and function of the hypaspists in Alexander's army, but other elements regarding them remain uncertain and have caused much discussion among scholars. The hypaspists formed a specialised unit of infantry soldiers that may possibly have been created by Philip. At the very least, they are mentioned already

---

6 Translation P.A. Brunt, Loeb 1976.
7 See Heckel 2013, 191–2; Hughes 2013, 136.
8 Waterfield 2011 assumes that he had been the commander since Nicanor's death in 330 (2011, 17). Heckel, on the other hand, considers Neoptolemus to have been Nicanor's successor (2013, 164). However, evidence for this does not really exist. Plutarch calls Neoptolemus *archihypaspist* (*Vit. Eum.* I.3), but it seems to me unlikely that he should have replaced Nicanor, since we hear nothing of him in Arrian's *Anabasis* after book II. An alternative scenario could be that no new leader of all hypaspists was appointed after Nicanor's death.

in relation to Alexander's campaign against the Thracians in spring 335 (Arr. *Anab* I.1.11); their purpose was to cover the flanks of the heavy phalanx and keep contact between the phalanx and the cavalry. Members of such a corps must have excelled in strength, speed and stamina; and these are qualities that Seleucus no doubt possessed, according to a later anecdote told by Appian (*Syr.* 57), which describes Seleucus as a man 'of such a large and powerful frame that once when a wild bull was brought for sacrifices to Alexander and broke loose from his ropes, Seleucus held him alone, with nothing but his hands, for which reason his statues are ornamented with horn'.[9] Although this anecdote was probably a much later explanation for depictions of Seleucus on coins and in sculpture with a bull's horns (see chapter 7 on ideology), he must indeed have been a man with a strong physique and very good health since Alexander appointed him commander of the royal hypaspists. We have neither a description nor a certain depiction of a hypaspist,[10] and we know little of the equipment of this corps, but they must have been more lightly armed than the phalangites. Instead of the heavy sarissa and large shield, they may have been armed with a shorter spear, a shield the size of the traditional Greek hoplon and, of course, a sword.

One of the uncertainties regarding the hypaspists is their organisation and their command structure. Arrian uses a number of terms. Thus we learn of hypaspists, hypaspists of the Companions, *agema* (corps or rather specific corps) of hypaspists and royal hypaspists. These terms probably derive from Ptolemy, and may reflect structural changes during the years of campaigning.[11] In the context of the battle at Granicus (spring 334), Arrian uses the term 'hypaspists of the Companions' (*Anab.* I.14.2);[12] while in relation to the battle at Issus (autumn 333) he mentions that on the right wing towards the mountain ridge Alexander, who himself fought here, placed first of the infantry the *agema* and hypaspists under Nicanor son of Parmenion' (*Anab.* II.8.3). In reporting the campaign in Asia, Arrian first uses the term in connection with the battle at Gaugamela (autumn 331): 'in the

---

9   Translation H. White, www.Perseus.tufts.edu.

10 Heckel considers a fighter in Greek armour and equipment fighting against a Persian on the Alexander sarcophagus to be a hypaspist (2013, fig. 7.1).

11 That such changes took place is confirmed by Arrian (*Anab.* III.16.9-11). During the winter of 331/330, new troops came to Susa from Macedonia, and, as a consequence, Alexander made some structural changes to his forces. He established two companies in each cavalry squadron, though there had never been cavalry companies previously, and named as their captains those among the Companions who had distinguished themselves in terms of bravery.

12 This is the only time that Arrian uses this term (Mensch's translation (2012) omits 'of the Companions').

Macedonian phalanx, *the agema*[13] of the hypaspists was posted right beside the cavalry and then the rest of the hypaspists; they were under Nicanor son of Parmenion' (*Anab*. III.11.9). When describing a later phase of the battle he mentions 'the royal hypaspists' (*Anab*. III.13.6), suggesting that they may have been identical with the *agema*. In these battles, the corps operated on the right wing next to the royal cavalry, which was directed by Alexander himself, while the left wing was under the command of Parmenion. The *agema*/the royal hypaspists served directly as Alexander's bodyguard and security force (there was also an *agema* of the cavalry in the army). In most of his narrative, Arrian (and probably Ptolemy) simply uses the term 'hypaspists' without further specification.

It is normally assumed that the corps consisted of 3,000 soldiers grouped in three chiliarchiai. Arrian uses the term chiliarchia in connection with hypaspists when reporting that Ptolemy was to take part of the army, including one chiliarchia of hypaspists, to track down Spitamenes in Sogdiana (*Anab*. III. 29.7). By the time Alexander's forces entered the territory of the Assacenians (probably winter 327/326), Nearchus and Antiochus are mentioned as chiliarchs of the hypaspists (*Anab*. IV.30.5). However, it is doubtful whether 3,000 was actually the number of hypaspists during the whole campaign or at any given time. If Antiochus was indeed given the task of leading three chiliarchiai of hypaspists, that would mean he led all the hypaspists. This seems unlikely, since none of them would then be available to follow Alexander, who was going down to the Indus to meet Hephaistion and Craterus.

As for the officers of the hypaspists, Nicanor is mentioned by Arrian as *hegemon*. He died of illness in the summer of 330 (Arr. *Anab*. III.25.4).[14] In *Anabasis* IV.30.5–6 (see above) the term used in connection with Antiochus and Nearchus is the verb *ago* (to lead). In the battle against Porus, Seleucus is also mentioned as leading the royal hypaspists (Arr. *Anab*. V.13.4). From the same passage we get the impression that the *agema* and the royal hypaspists were, in fact, not the same: 'next to the cavalry he [Alexander] marshalled from the infantry the royal hypaspists under Seleucus, then the royal *agema*, and next the rest of the hypaspists'; in general, it seems that Arrian sometimes confuses the terms for different parts of the armed forces.

---

13 *Agema* is first used by Arrian in connection with Alexander's campaign against the Thracians (*Anab*. I.1.11).

14 Heckel (2013, 164) suggests that Neoptolemus succeeded Nicanor as general of the hypaspists, since Plutarch refers to him as *archihypaspist* (*Vit. Eum.* I.3). This is unlikely, since in Arrian's *Anabasis* Neoptolemus disappears after book II, though the hypaspists play an important role in the remaining campaigns.

In battles on terrain where the cavalry would be of no use, such as the battle against the army of Sagalassos (334–3), the hypaspists fought on the right wing with Alexander (Arr. *Anab*. I.28.4).

During the early years of Alexander's campaign, Seleucus may also have participated in operations in which the hypaspists must have excelled, such as the siege of Tyre. Here they were with Alexander (together with some of the cavalry squadrons, the Agrianians and the archers) destroying smaller sites near the Antilebanon, and at Tyre itself we find hypaspists on one of the ships attacking Tyre from the sea, mounting the wall with Alexander and later fighting with the king inside the city walls. The slaughter was great, according to Arrian, and 20 of the hypaspists lost their lives on this occasion (*Anab*. II.20.6). At Gaza, Alexander took the hypaspists with him and rushed to the support of the Macedonians when Arab mercenaries made a sortie from the city, severely threatening the Macedonians siege forces (Arr. *Anab*. II.27.1). After Issus, Seleucus was probably in Egypt; the hypaspists are mentioned specifically sailing down the Nile from Memphis to the sea (Arr. *Anab*. III.1.4).

In Arrian's *Anabasis* the hypaspists are mentioned more often in connection with Alexander's military operations after the battle at Gaugamela. This may be a coincidence or reflect that more operations needed the special skills of this section of the forces, i.e. operating as vanguard in difficult terrain, where cavalry would be of little or no use, and where Alexander himself fought on foot. This begins after the stay in Susa during the winter of 331/330, in relation to conflicts with the Ouxioi living in the mountains east of the Pasitigris river (Arr. *Anab*. III.17), then in relation to the subsequent Battle of the Persian Gates against Ariobarzanes during the conquest of Persepolis, when Alexander took a small portion of his forces, including the hypaspists, on a path around the Gates to launch a surprise attack on the enemy at dawn. Hypaspists were also used in the final pursuit of Bessus (who held Darius as prisoner), during which Ptolemy was made responsible for hunting him down (Arr. *Anab*. III.29.7). Among the troops allocated to him was, as mentioned above, a chiliarchia of hypaspists. In book IV, covering the campaigns in Bactria, Sogdiana and the mountains of northwestern India where several sieges and attacks on cities, but no regular battles, took place, the hypaspists' role as crack troops becomes increasingly evident.

On their way down the Hydaspes in the autumn of 326, after the battle against Porus and the agreement with him, Alexander divided the army. Under his own command he placed all the hypaspists, the archers and the Agrianians, and the cavalry *agema* (Arr. *Anab*. VI.2.2.). When he reached the Acesinus river, Alexander took the hypaspists, the archers, the Agria-

Fig. 2 | *The tomb of*
Cyrus, Pasagardae,
north of Persepolis.

nians, Peithon's battalion of so-called asthetairoi, all the mounted bow-
men and half the Companion cavalry, and marched across a waterless
region against the Malloi, one of the autonomous Indian tribes; this was
a campaign that nearly cost Alexander his life and left him very seriously
wounded (Arr. *Anab.* VI.10–11).

We do not know if Seleucus participated in the march through the
Gedrosia desert, which may well have been the hardest section of the
whole Asian campaign, or whether he was with Craterus on the easier
inland route back through eastern Iran. However, Arrian reports that Alexander took with him half the hypaspists (*Anab.* VI.22.1), which might suggest that Seleucus, as the leader of the royal hypaspists, was indeed with
him. In the winter of 325–324, these two portions of Alexander's forces met
up in Carmania. Later that winter it is probable that Seleucus was with
Alexander during the move to Pasargadae (being among 'the most mobile
foot soldiers') and witnessed how Alexander had the tomb of Cyrus – which

had been desecrated and plundered – restored again to its original condition (Arr. *Anab.* VI.29.4-8). If this was indeed the case, this could be one of probably many events that contributed to Seleucus' understanding of the importance of upholding the local traditions and heritage of conquered peoples.

In the spring of 324, the army was in Susa, and here the famous mass wedding of soldiers to Persian women in Persian style took place. Arrian tells of the wedding that Alexander held for himself and his Companions with the daughters of the highest-ranking Persians and Medes (*Anab.* VII.4.4-6). The names of the Companions listed by Arrian are Hephaistion, Craterus, Perdiccas, Ptolemy, Eumenes, Nearchus and Seleucus. Arrian adds that other Companions were also married, altogether totaling about 80, and that more than 10,000 soldiers were listed as married to Persian women.

After the events in Susa, Alexander sailed down the Eulaeus with the hypaspists, the *agema* (it is not specified which *agema*) and a few cavalry Companions (Arr. *Anab.* VII.7.1). From the estuary of the Eulaeus, he sailed along the Persian coast to the mouth of the Tigris and continued up this river to Opis. Here Alexander gave a speech in which he announced that those no longer fit for active service were to be discharged and returned to Macedonia, whilst those who continued with him would receive so much that their rewards would cause envy in Macedonia and stir up other Macedonians to come and serve under him. This speech must have caused deep resentment among many of the soldiers present, and a sense that Alexander held them in contempt. The reaction to it was that they all wanted to be discharged from the army, saying that Alexander could continue his campaign with his father, Ammon. As leader of the royal hypaspists Seleucus probably participated in this part of Alexander's last sailing trip, and we may assume that he was involved in leading away the 13 men whom Alexander wanted executed due to the protests against his speech. Alexander had those who cried most loudly and protested most vehemently arrested, pointing out personally which men the hypaspists were to arrest and execute.

The last time we meet Seleucus in Arrian's *Anabasis* is in the summer of 323, in the desperate days before Alexander's death in Babylon. According to Arrian, he used here the so-called Royal Diaries, *Ephemerides*, as his source (*Anab.* VII.26.2).[15]

---

15 For a recent discussion of these, see Romm and Mensch 2011, Appendices A and P. Plutarch stresses that his account of Alexander's death (*Life of Alexander*) is taken from the *Royal Diaries*.

'The Royal Journals say that Peithon, Attalus, Demophon and Peucestas, with Cleomenes, Menidas and Seleucus, slept in the temple of Serapis[16] enquiring of the god whether it would be more desirable and better for Alexander to be brought into the temple of the god and after supplication to receive care of the god, but that an oracle was given from the god that he should not be brought into the temple, and that it would be better for him to stay where he was, and that, shortly after the Companions announced this, Alexander died; so it was in fact this that was now "better".' (Arr. *Anab.* VII.26.2)

Arrian states that Aristobulus and Ptolemy recorded no more than this, but adds that some have recorded that when asked by his Companions to whom he would leave his kingdom he replied "To the best/strongest man" (*Anab.* VII.26.3). Neither Arrian nor Plutarch mention what other sources report;[17] that is, that he gave his signet ring to Perdiccas.

---

16 This has often been commented on as being an error, and that the link with the Serapis cult was invented by Ptolemy long after Alexander's death. However, to me the reference to Serapis might indicate that the source on which Arrian relied was Egyptian. Could it indicate that these journals were edited later in Alexandria or simply that the original Babylonian god was 'translated' by Arrian to a god well known to the Romans?

17 Diod. Sic. XVII.117.39; Quintus Curtius X.5.4; Justin XII.15.12.

CHAPTER 2

The death of Alexander
and the first struggles
for power

Alexander died on the afternoon of 11 June 323, according to the *Astronomical Diaries*.[1] The days of confusion following his death left the army in chaos. It became more obvious than ever that, despite resentment bubbling up on a number of occasions, it was Alexander himself who had kept both the expedition and the army together. Our main literary sources for the drama that ensued in Babylon[2] differ in details but more or less agree on the main events. The aim here is not to discuss the events of these fateful days in detail,[3] but to attempt to follow what happened to Seleucus.

A meeting of the most senior officers ended with an agreement to wait for Alexander's wife, Roxane, to give birth; if the child was a boy, he would be elected king.[4] The cavalry accepted this, but the infantry was of a different opinion and wanted Alexander's half-brother Arrhidaeus to succeed him, even though he suffered from a mental disability. The phalanx of the infantry was supporting Arrhidaeus, son of Philip, for the kingship, though he was afflicted with an incurable mental illness. An armed conflict seemed close, and the most influential of the Friends and of the Bodyguard, together with the cavalry, decided to send envoys of whom the

---

1   *Astronomical Diaries* 1–322B, mentioning 'the king died'; see Boiy 2004, 116–7; 2013, 10.
2   Arr. *Events*; Diod. Sic. XVIII.1.2; Pompeius Trogus (Justin 13.2-4); Curtius X.6 (a much more elaborate and highly colourful version); Plut. *Vit. Eum.* III.1 (Eumenes stayed with the army rather than with the groups of high-ranking officers; according to Plutarch, this was because Eumenes considered this to be the most suitable arrangement; however, it is probably more likely that the officers did not issue him with an invitation to join them); Dexippos *FGrH* 100.8.
3   Hammond and Walbank 1988, 95ff; Romm 2012, chapter 2; Waterfield 2011, chapter 2.
4   Pompeius Trogus and particularly Curtius include what must be considered fanciful discussions among those present at the meeting. Thus Pompeius Trogus records that Meleager – and Curtius that Nearchus – brought Heracles, a son of Alexander by Barsine, into the discussion, and that Ptolemy opted for decisions agreed by the generals or their majority, since neither Heracles nor Roxane's unborn child were full-blooded Macedonians, having mothers who were Persian, and thus neither was worthy to rule their conquerors, the Macedonians.

most prominent was Meleager to the infantry and demand submission to their orders. Meleager, however, did not ask the phalanx for submission, but instead he incited the phalanx to stick to their resolution and ended up being chosen as the leader of the Macedonians. At some point, the Bodyguard and the cavalry withdrew from Babylon. A confrontation was thus avoided, and it was agreed to make both Arrhidaeus (under the name Philip [III]) and Roxane's child – if a son – kings, and to appoint Perdiccas *epimeletes* (regent). It was further agreed that the most important of the Friends and the Bodyguard should take over the satrapies and obey the king and Perdiccas.

With order restored, the 30 infantry soldiers who had protested the strongest were executed, and Meleager too was punished (Diod. Sic. XVIII.4.7). Perdiccas, after taking council from the most important officers, decided to distribute the satrapies.[5] Antipater received Macedonia and neighbouring areas.[6] Of Seleucus' later rivals, Ptolemy was given Egypt and Lysimachus was awarded Thrace in Europe along with the neighbouring area near the Pontic Sea. Antigonus, whom Alexander had left in charge of Phrygia in 333, seems not to have been present at the negotiations in Babylon, but he was clearly, even at a distance, a figure to be reckoned with and was given Pamphylia, Lycia and Great Phrygia. Leonnatus was given Hellespontine Phrygia. Peithon, a close ally of Seleucus for some years, was given Media, whilst Peucestas was awarded Persia. Babylonia, which Seleucus was to receive later, was given to Archon and Mesopotamia to Archelaus. Also among those chosen as satraps at the meeting was Eumenes, who received Paphlagonia and Cappadocia, and who was to play an important role in Seleucus' life in future years. Clearly, the highest-ranking generals received the satrapies in the west, those close to the Mediterranean.

Seleucus did not receive a satrapy, but Perdiccas chose him as commander of the cavalry of the Companions. In his account, Diodorus Siculus (XVIII.3.4) adds that this was 'a most distinguished office; for Hephaistion commanded them first, Perdiccas after him, and the third the above-named Seleucus'.[7] This appointment indicates that there was a good relationship between the two men and also that Perdiccas was convinced of the soldiers' trust in Seleucus and of his talent as commander; but it also

---

5   Listed by Diod. Sic. XVIII.3; Arr. *Events*; Curtius X.X.1–4.
6   According to Arrian's *Events after Alexander* 7, this was in partnership with Craterus, who by the time of Alexander's death was in Cilicia en route to Macedonia to replace Antipater and bring back veteran soldiers to Macedonia.
7   Curtius does not mention Seleucus in connection with the meeting in Babylon.

indicates that Seleucus did not hold, at this point, a high enough position to warrant offering him a satrapy. The meeting in Babylon thus resulted in Seleucus staying with the main army under Perdiccas, and, in this way, he stayed very close to the heart of the action over the course of the coming years. Had he been awarded a satrapy in the east, Seleucus may well have missed out on the opportunities that the position of commander of the Companions allowed. The position also allowed him to display his talents and demonstrate his ambitions, resulting in his ascent to become one of the main players in the series of events that led up to the first confrontation between the Diadochs. The following more than 20 years would teach him at first hand, if he did not already know, how ambitious men and women interacted in a world of more or less hidden agendas and broken alliances.

After the agreement in Babylon, Peithon was sent east, on Perdiccas' order, to crush the revolt of the Greek settlers in the upper satrapies that had broken out when the news of Alexander's death had reached them. With this mission accomplished, he then returned to Perdiccas and the army at Babylon (Diod. Sic. XVIII.3.3, 4.8). Peithon was clearly a person of more importance than Seleucus, but he and Seleucus were apparently, if not friends, then at least on very good terms, and they became the most significant figures in Perdiccas' royal army.

When Perdiccas left Babylon with the main army and the kings Philip III (Arrhidaeus) and Alexander IV (Roxane's son, probably born in August 323), he clearly saw it as his responsibility, as *epimeletes*, to secure and stabilise the realm that Alexander had created. His first move was against Ariarathes, the king of Cappadocia; this was a region that Alexander had bypassed when pursuing Darius and the Persian army eastwards. Ariarathes (Diod. Sic. XVIII.161; Arr. *Events* X) had refused to hand over his kingdom to Eumenes. After Perdiccas had defeated him, and had him executed, Eumenes was installed as satrap as had been agreed in Babylon the previous year.

Next, Perdiccas moved the army south into Pisidia. This may simply have been undertaken with the aim of finding better conditions for the large army; however, it turned into an expedition of punishment. Two cities were laid waste after the inhabitants had killed the Macedonian general Balacrus appointed by Alexander as satrap. First the city of the Larandians was destroyed and then that of the Isaurians. On the third day of the siege of the latter, when their situation was desperate, the defenders decided not to surrender but to gather their families in their houses and set fire to them, and then, after continuing to fight to the end, they threw themselves on the pyres into which their homes had been transformed. The next morning Perdiccas gave the city to his soldiers as booty. According to Diodorus

Siculus, much gold and silver was found here (Diod. Sic. XVIII.4–8). The brutality that characterised much of Alexander's campaign in the east thus continued undiminished under Perdiccas' command. Nonetheless, providing booty as payment to the soldiers was essential in order to keep up their fighting spirit and maintain their loyalty.

Before the campaign against Cappadocia, Perdiccas had asked for support from at least two satraps – Leonnatus and Antigonus[8] – but neither responded. Leonnatus had instead gone to Macedonia and Greece, under the pretext of assisting Antipater in the Lamian War but really in an attempt to marry Cleopatra, a sister of Alexander who was the widow of Alexander, King of Epirus. He was soon afterwards killed in a battle against the Athenians. Antigonus seems simply to have ignored Perdiccas' call. The latter's move into Pisidia and probably his presence in Cappadocia was no doubt seen by Antigonus as a threat to his own power base in Asia Minor. Arrian suggests that Perdiccas was conspiring against Antigonus (*Events* I.20). Certainly by now, a year after Alexander's death, the majority of the most senior of Alexander's officers clearly began to see the opportunities that might open up for them. Since Alexander's death, Perdiccas had kept close contact with Antipater in Macedonia, and, like many of the others, he had attempted to secure his position by a favourable marriage alliance. By this time, he had secured Antipater's consent to marry one of his three daughters,[9] Nicaea. After the death of Alexander, most of the senior officers had apparently divorced their Persian wives – one exception being Seleucus – and were now busy competing to obtain a prestigious Macedonian wife.

Perdiccas ordered Antigonus to come to the army camp in order to explain why he had not responded to Perdiccas' call to join him against Ariarathes, or, as Diodorus Siculus, whose sympathy is clearly with Antigonus (XVIII.23.4), puts it, to defend himself against Perdiccas' slander and unjust charges. Antigonus, however, soon fled from the camp with his son Demetrius and went to Antipater with a story about Perdiccas' plans to marry, not Antipater's daughter Nicaea, but Alexander's own sister Cleopatra, as well as his ambitions to secure the Macedonian kingship. Antipater and Craterus seem to have believed Antigonus, or, at the very least, they became sufficiently suspicious to launch a campaign against Perdiccas in Asia.

Back at the army camp, Perdiccas now (autumn 321) asked his friends and generals, among whom Seleucus must have been a leading figure, if

---

8   Plut. *Vit.Eum* III.

9   About the same time, another of the daughters, Phila, was married to Craterus, who had returned to Europe in order to support Antipater. Eurydice, the third daughter, married Ptolemy, probably after Triparadeisus.

they should march against Macedonia or first against Ptolemy in Egypt (Diod. Sic. XVIII.25.6); they decided that the priority was to defeat Ptolemy. According to Arrian, he took this course of action despite the opposition of the army (*Events* XIX). The reason for marching against Ptolemy was that Arrhidaeus, the officer who was in charge of Alexander's funeral procession from Babylon to Aigai (Pausanias 1.6.3), had travelled to Egypt against Perdiccas' wishes (Arr. *Events* XVI); he probably took this course of action because Ptolemy had gone to Syria with an army and directed the funeral train to Alexandria, where he had taken responsibility for the interment of Alexander's body and ultimately placed the sarcophagus in Alexandria (Diod. Sic. XIII.28.3) or Memphis (Pausanius I.6.3; Curtius X.X.20, who adds that he transferred it to Alexandria a few years later).

Before Perdiccas marched against Egypt, he had given Eumenes the task, supported by a separate force, of preventing Antipater and Craterus from crossing the Hellespont. During the course of the subsequent battle (described in detail by Diod. Sic. XVIII.31), which was to be the first between the Diadochs, Craterus was killed in a fall from his horse and Neoptolemus was killed by Eumenes in a duel. Thus two of Alexander's top generals were dead, and a third was soon to follow.

Arrian (*Events* XIX) describes Perdiccas' Egyptian campaign very briefly: 'He was defeated twice, and, having treated those who were inclined to go over to Ptolemy with great severity, and in other respects behaved in the camp more arrogantly than became a general, he was slain by his own cavalry during an engagement.' According to the detailed account of Diodorus (XVIII.33), Perdiccas' campaign against Ptolemy brought the royal army from Damascus first to Pelusium, where, apparently during the clearing of an old branch of a canal, water suddenly poured into the canal and caused alarm amongst the army. Many of Perdiccas' friends deserted him and went over to Ptolemy. At this point, Diodorus digresses with a comparison of the evil character of Perdiccas – a man of blood and tyrannical disposition – with that of Ptolemy, who was considered generous and fair and who let all commanders speak freely. Ptolemy sensibly, however, relied not only on the excellence of his own character but also on having garrisoned, with large forces, all the important sites of Egypt.

Perdiccas made a second attempt to cross the Nile, after behaving in a very friendly manner towards his men; by offering gifts and promises, he inspired them to join him. After a night march at top speed, the forces camped on the bank of the Nile opposite a fortress called the Camel Fort. At dawn, Perdiccas commenced sending his troops across the river with elephants in the vanguard; he followed with the hypaspists, the ladder-carriers and others he planned to use in an attack against the fortress. At the rear came the bravest of the cavalry forces, whom he planned to send against Ptolemy' troops, if they appeared. Ptolemy, with his best men, was actually defending the fortress and had the advantage of higher ground. Perdiccas had more men, but, after a day's fighting, he gave up the siege and went back to his camp. Later, he again set out on a night march to a point on the Nile opposite Memphis, where there was an island in the river big enough to hold a large camp. The location must have seemed ideal, and the men started to cross the river. This, however, turned out to be difficult, since the water came up to their chins and they started to drift down the river. Perdiccas attempted to stop this by placing elephants in a line across the river upstream and, on the other side of the crossing men, he placed horsemen who were able to pick up those who the current carried away. What seemed a solid plan actually turned the situation into a disaster. The presence in the river of elephants, horses and men resulted in the river becoming deeper and deeper, as the sand on the riverbed was carried away down river by the strong movements of the water. Thus only part of the army was able to cross, and Perdiccas decided to recall those troops who had already reached the island, resulting in the drowning of a great many men, whilst others were devoured by wild animals, according to Diodorus Siculus (XVIII.35.6).

Fig. 3 | *The pediment of one short end of the so-called Alexander sarcophagus presenting a scene often interpreted as the murder of Perdiccas. The sarcophagus, together with three other monumental sarcophagi, was found in the Royal Tomb at Sidon and is most often identified as belonging to Abdalonymus, appointed King of Sidon by Alexander.*

More than 2,000 men were lost, including high-ranking officers. Any remaining trust in Perdiccas' abilities as a general who could bring victory was now lost, and replaced by anger. During the night, the camp was filled with lamentations and mourning. Particularly horrifying, according to Diodorus Siculus (XVIII.36.3), was the fact that about half the men had been eaten by wild beasts. Ptolemy organised proper funeral rites for the bodies that were washed ashore on the other side of the Nile, and sent the bones to the relatives and friends of the dead. Of course, Ptolemy himself and/or some of his men may well have known several of the drowned officers personally, and thus it was probably the bones of these officers that were sent home.

By now, Perdiccas had completely lost control of his troops. According to Diodorus Siculus, many of the generals joined in the accusations being hurled at Perdiccas, and the phalanx made their hostility towards him clear with threatening shouts (XVIII.36.4). 'Consequently about a hundred of the commanders were the first to revolt from him, of whom the most illustrious was Peithon, who had suppressed the rebellious Greeks in the Upper Satrapies, a man second to none of the Companions of Alexander, in courage and reputation; next also some of the cavalry conspired together and went to the tent of Perdiccas, where they fell on him in a body and stabbed him to death' (Diod. Sic. XVIII.36.5). However, as noted above, according

to Arrian (*Events* XIX), Perdiccas 'was slain by his own cavalry during an engagement'.[10] This description of his death is difficult to equate with the development of Perdiccas' Egyptian campaign as described by Diodorus.

In any case, Seleucus is not mentioned explicitly by Diodorus, but it cannot be doubted that he took part in the mutiny, being Perdiccas' cavalry commander, and thus *de facto* second in command, and apparently on friendly terms with Peithon. The only source that mentions Seleucus specifically is Cornelius Nepos in his biography of Eumenes (V.1). He states that Perdiccas was killed by Antigenes[11] and Seleucus. Memnon (IV) mentions

---

10 Translation J.H. Freese, https://www.livius.org/.
11 Antigenes' role is confirmed by Diod. Sic. XVIII.39.6 where he states that Antigenes was given Susiana 'because he had been foremost in making the attack on Perdiccas'.

in passing, when presenting Dionysius of Heraclea and his history, that Perdiccas was a poor leader and was killed by his men.

By now, Peithon and Seleucus must have been the principal figures of the royal army. However, Ptolemy's power and prestige had increased too – and Alexander's body remained in Egypt. In many ways Ptolemy benefitted most from the mutiny of Perdiccas' officers, and he probably had close contact with some of Perdiccas' men, such as Peithon and Seleucus. By showing magnanimity, visiting the camp of the royal army and sending grain, he also secured the army's confidence. Peithon's prestige relied on his having been one of Alexander's Bodyguards (*somatophylakes*) and also on being appointed satrap of Media at the meeting in Babylon and his successful crushing of the Greek revolt in Bactria after Alexander's death. Thus it was now Peithon who was elected guardian of the kings and supreme commander of the army, together with Arrhidaeus, who had brought Alexander's funeral procession to Egypt.

Ironically, during these fatal days in Egypt, Perdiccas' ally Eumenes won a victory over Craterus and Neoptolemus (see above). When news of this reached the camp of the main army in Egypt 'immediately' after Perdiccas' death, according to Diodorus Siculus (XVIII.37) it resulted in the army passing a death sentence upon Eumenes and 50 of his men, among them Perdiccas' brother Alcetas. And, to be on the safe side, Perdiccas' most faithful friends and his sister Atalante, wife of Attalus, the man who had received the command of the fleet, were immediately killed. Attalus, who had been waiting with the fleet at Pelusium, sailed to Tyre, where he stayed and received friends of Perdiccas, who had escaped from the camp at Memphis. The royal army, with the two kings and their new guardians, moved north along the coast of Phoenicia.

Triparadeisus: a new agreement

In the late summer/early autumn of 320,[12] Antipater, who had crossed the Hellespont with Craterus, came to Triparadeisus (the triple 'paradise') in Syria, where the army was camped. This was clearly a large estate from Achaemenid times, but its precise location is not known – Baalbek has been suggested by Schlumberger (1969). By the time of Antipater's arrival, the army was in disarray; two factions were fighting for decisive influence.

---

12 Diodorus dates the meeting to 321, Mamor Parium to 320 as does the Babylonian sources. Scholars have discussed the date, and most consider 320 as the correct year; see e.g. Anson 2002/2003. See also chapter 3.

Eurydice, one of the enterprising Macedonian princesses who had made her way, together with her mother, to Asia and had married king Philip despite opposition from Perdiccas,[13] was now busy stirring up resentments. She apparently managed to turn the army against Peithon and Arrhidaeus to such an extent that they both took the surprising step of resigning as guardians of the kings. Thus Antipater, who was by now nearly 80 years old, was met by troops who were hardly in the mood to listen to him. According to Arrian (*Events* I.22), he only escaped being killed thanks to Antigonus and Seleucus intervening, at great risk to their own lives. Although the royal army had so clearly turned against Peithon, the troops apparently viewed Seleucus as an officer they could trust. Antigonus' presence in the camp must have been due to a planned meeting with Antipater. Diodorus Siculus (XVIII.39.4) states only that there was a tumult, which Antipater stopped by addressing the troops and by frightening Eurydice.

In any case, the meeting at Triparadeisus was the occasion at which Seleucus joined the exclusive top group of Macedonian officers. As a consequence of a redistribution of satrapies, Seleucus rose to a new level of power. He was elevated from being Perdiccas' second in command to being satrap of the rich region of Babylonia, replacing Docimus, who was Perdiccas' man and must have been among those officers condemned at Triparadeisus.[14] Docimus[15] had been appointed satrap of Babylonia by Perdiccas, in place of Archon, and must have been with the royal army when it set out from Babylon. Thus, Seleucus' role at the meeting at Triparadeisus and his part in removing Perdiccas provided him with this new opportunity as satrap of Babylonia. Antigenes was given the neighbouring satrapy of Susiana, according to Diodorus Siculus (XVIII.39.5), 'because he had been foremost in making the attack on Perdiccas'. Peithon was reinstated as satrap of Media. Arrhidaeus was given Hellespontine Phrygia. The man who gained the most at Triparadeisus, however, was Antigonus; he was now

---

13 See Arr. *Events* I.15; Polyaenos *Stratagems* VIII.60.

14 Alexander on his first stay in Babylon had reinstated Mazaeus as satrap, with Apollodorus of Amphipolis as commander of the troops. Mazaeus died in 328 and, according to Arrian (*Anab.* IV.18.3): 'Later when he learnt that Mazaios had died, Alexander appointed Stamenes (only mentioned by Arrian in this connection). Apollodorus still held his position on the return of Alexander to Babylon after the campaign in India. When Perdiccas assigned the satrapies after Alexander's death, Archon of Pella was appointed satrap of Babylonia (Diod. Sic. XVIII.3). Later, Pediccas replaced him with Docimus (see chapter 3).

15 He was among the officers who, together with Perdiccas' brother Alketas, were assigned to join Eumenes against Craterus and Antipater when Perdiccas set out for Egypt. Later, he was taken prisoner in Pisidia after Antigonus' battle against Alketas. He reappears in Diodorus Siculus' narrative a couple of years later (XIX.16), when, together with a group of officers with whom he was captured, he managed to take over the fortress where he was being held prisoner. He succeeded in making contact with Stratonice, wife of Antigonus, who was in the vicinity, but was caught by Antigonus' men when he tried to escape from the fortress.

appointed general of the royal army and given the task of hunting down Eumenes. The two kings, with their families, accompanied Antipater back to Macedonia, while Antipater's son Cassander was appointed second in command to Antigonus (i.e. he took over Seleucus' former role in the royal army).

The meeting at Triparadeisus was both an end and a beginning. Within three years of Alexander's death, Perdiccas, to whom Alexander allegedly gave his ring, had been murdered by his own officers and Craterus and Leonnatus had been killed on the battlefield. Ptolemy, on the other hand, had strengthened his position as satrap of Egypt and been given additional areas west of Egypt, such as Cyrenaica, which he had actually already conquered. Lysimachus, who did not participate in the meeting, is not included in Diodorus Siculus' list but continued as satrap of Thrace; he had by this time married Antipater's daughter Nicaea, who had been married briefly to Perdiccas. It was most likely shortly after Triparadeisus that Eurydice, another of Antipater's daughters, married Ptolemy. His third daughter, Phila, had been married to Craterus and was probably now[16] married to Antigonus' considerably younger son, Demetrius (Poliorketes). Antipater's marriage policy for his daughters clearly reflects that it was those satraps close to Macedonia and Greece that he worried about; in his worldview, those of the distant satrapies were of little importance. He had not participated in Alexander's Asian campaigns, but rather stayed in Macedonia and looked after things there; he was now 80 years old and the Mediterranean region remained his focal point.

---

16 Rather than later, as is sometimes assumed, because she spread Craterus' ashes in 315/314.

CHAPTER 3

Satrap of Babylonia

Seleucus probably left Triparadeisus as quickly as possible after being appointed satrap of Babylonia; he may have travelled with other eastern satraps such as Peithon (Media), Antigenes (Susiana) and Amphimachus (Mesopotamia and Arbelitis), who later joined Eumenes in the Second Diadoch War, until the crossing of the Euphrates in northern Syria. Seleucus disappears from the preserved Greco-Roman literary sources for the next couple of years; he reappears when the struggle between Eumenes and Antigonus moved eastwards with Eumenes' first appearance in Mesopotamia in 317.

Perdiccas had at some point in 321 sent Docimus to replace Archon, who had been appointed satrap of Babylonia after Alexander's death. The two men fought,[1] and though Archon seems to have had the support of the local people, he lost the battle and was killed. The *Babylonian Chronicle of Diadochi*[2] mentions an appointment as 'satrap of Akkad' (line 22); this probably refers to Docimus, rather than Seleucus.[3] Line 25 notes that 'the satrap of Akkad entered Babylon'; this must refer to Seleucus, though no name is mentioned. He probably entered Babylon late in 319. Before the arrival of Seleucus, Docimus had already fled to Eumenes, when it became clear that the supporters of Perdiccas were to be punished.

The *Chronicle* also offers the following information. Lines 26–7: Philip year 5 (319/318):

'The king [left] Antigon[us in charge of …] and he [i.e. the king] went to the land of Macedonia and did not return. In a later part? [of the year? …]'.

---

1   Arr. *Events* Cod. Vatic. Gr 495, fol 230r; Schober 1981; Agostinetti 1993. BCHP 3; translation R.J. van der Spek, https://www.livius.org/sources/about/mesopotamian-chronicles/
2   BCHP 3; translation R.J. van der Spek, https://www.livius.org/sources/about/mesopotamian-chronicles/
3   See, e.g., Anson 2002/2003.

Line 28 (319/18):

'After that (the lines?) are destroyed. Fire consumed it. Seleucus the satrap [of Akkad …]'.

As satrap of Babylonia, Seleucus took up his first major administrative task. He had gained a rich and important province, linking the western and the eastern parts of Alexander's empire; and this was a region with which he was already familiar from his time with Alexander and the period after his death, when Seleucus had remained in Babylon with Perdiccas and the army. Thus, he already knew the geography and the climate, the main routes through the region, the waterways and the roads. He must have had at least some knowledge of the economy and also of religion and social structures. Following his appointment as satrap, he had about two years in which to expand his knowledge of the region and get a firm grip on the province before war moved to Mesopotamia and Babylonia when Eumenes invaded Babylonia in 317 on his way east, pursued by Antigonus. Of Alexander's high-ranking officers, Seleucus was perhaps the most talented at understanding the importance of logistics and the options available within a given region. During the Babylonian War (see below) he and his general Patrocles efficiently exploited the Babylonian landscape with its flood plains and irrigation systems.

In the autumn of 317, Eumenes was being hard pressed by Antigonus,[4] following the breaking of his pledge of loyalty to the latter, and he moved east in the hope of assistance from the eastern satraps. He crossed the Euphrates with an army of 4,000 cavalry and 20,000 light-infantry troops, including the famous Silver Shields (Diod. Sic. XVIII.73).[5] During the winter of 317/316, Eumenes and his army made camp in Carian villages in Babylonia (Diod. Sic. XIX.12).[6] He sent envoys to Peithon[7] and Seleucus asking them to support the kings[8] and join him in the struggle against Antigonus. Seleucus' response is frequently quoted: he was willing to be of service to the kings but not to carry out orders from Eumenes, whom the Macedonian army assembly had condemned to death at Triparadeisus. The discussions developed to a point where Seleucus and Peithon sent an ambassador to Antigenes (and the Silver Shields) asking him to remove Eumenes from the command. Antigenes and his elite troops remained unpersuaded by the arguments of Seleucus and Peithon, and Eumenes marched to the Tigris and made camp about 300 stades (ca. 60 km) from Babylon. He intended to move to Susa to summon the armies of the Upper Satrapies and in order to have access to the wealth of the treasury in the city's citadel. However,

---

4   Meeus 2012, 74-96.
5   Antigenes, who had been the first to stab Perdiccas in his tent (chapter 2) and appointed satrap of Susiana at Triparadeisus, had been asked to transfer part of the treasure at Susa to Cyinda with the Macedonian Silver Shields. At Cyinda they were persuaded to join Eumenes by means of a letter that Polyperchon (a Macedonian general who had participated in Alexander's anabasis, and whom Antipater had appointed regent and supreme commander at his deathbed, thus surpassing his own son Cassander) and the kings had sent to Eumenes (Diod. Sic. XVIII.58-59).
6   For the problems of identifying these specific villages, see Potts 2018. There seem to have been several villages of Carians in Babylonia. The Carian villages mentioned here are tentatively situated by Potts in the Nippur district; to date, this identification remains uncertain.
7   Peithon, the satrap of Media, had put to death Philotas, the former general of Parthia, and replaced him with his own brother. The other eastern satraps clearly feared sharing Philotas' fate and therefore joined forces. A battle with Peithon did take place, as a result of which Peithon withdrew to Media; some time later, he went to Babylon to make an alliance with Seleucus.
8   Eumenes had been asked by Polyperchon and Olympias, now guardians of the kings, to fight against Antigonus, whom they saw as a rebel. Therefore, Eumenes' army was at that time the royal army. See also note 51.

he was forced to cross the river since the country behind him had been plundered and could not provide food for the troops.[9]

BCHP 3 lines 33–7, month VII (3–31 October 317), which are very fragmentary, seem to refer to a fight between the royal troops (i.e. Eumenes' army) and the satrap (Seleucus) at the palace – suggesting that Eumenes came to Babylon – and that later the satrap destroyed the fence of reed.[10] Boiy (2010) suggests that the Babylonian scribe responsible for these lines was not aware which group actually comprised the royal troops and that this passage is concerned with Antigonus, because, by the high chronology, Eumenes should at this time have been in Iran.

Line 36 states:

'the Macedonians of the king in order to make a strong guard between …';

and line 37:

'[Lat]er Antigonus … the satrap [of Babylonia …]'. Then, for year 316/315, month IV (25 June to 24 July): 'Antig[onus … the satrap'; the next line: 'who [was] in the palace of the king, whi[ch …'.

Boiy thus suggests the low chronology from the Babylonian texts and the Marmor Parium for Triparadeisus, but now a change to the high chronology of Diodorus Siculus. The central question here is actually the length of time of two periods: (1) between Triparadeisus and Eumenes' arrival in Babylonia and the length of his stay there[11] and (2) the length of the campaign in Iran.

According to the low chronology, Eumenes stayed in Babylonia for a fairly long time. Diodorus Siculus (XIX.13) tells us that Eumenes wanted to continue to Susa and that his troops managed to get hold of boats for the crossing, but that Seleucus and Peithon sailed downstream in two triremes and many punts, and again attempted to persuade Antigenes and his men 'not to go against their own interests and to prefer a foreigner who had

---

9   Grainger (1990, 39) suggests that he was in the area before harvest time, and that this explains why there were not enough supplies. The lack of provisions may also have been due to the fact that Eumenes and his army had spent a great deal of time in Babylonia, including over the winter.

10 For a detailed exposition of these lines and their meaning, see Boiy 2010, 1-13, where he discusses the editions of various scholars in detail. I have chosen to use the most recent translation: Finkel and van der Spek online = BCHP 3 https:/www.livius.org/sources/about/mesopotamian-chronicles/.

11 Note that the Marmor Parium continues the low chronology from Triparadeisus when dating the naval victory of Cleitus on behalf of Polyperchon against Nicanor, Antigonus' general, which took place near Byzantium. Diodorus Siculus dates it to 318, Marmor Parium to 317/316.

killed many Macedonians'. Once again, they did not succeed.[12] Seleucus, who had by now clearly learnt how to wage warfare in the Babylonian landscape, sailed off to an old canal that had become filled over time and had it cleared out. As a consequence, the camp of the stubborn Macedonians was quickly surrounded by water and in danger of being completely inundated. On the second day, Eumenes' men managed to get hold of about 300 punts and carried across most of the troops while Seleucus' forces did nothing to prevent their landing. Diodorus Siculus claims this was due to Seleucus having only cavalry troops with him and these in much inferior numbers to Eumenes. However, as night fell, Eumenes began to worry about the baggage train and got his men back across the river; there, with the help of a native, he conducted excavations so as to drain away the water and make the surrounding land passable. Seleucus now displayed one of his strongest talents: the ability to bide his time. He negotiated a truce with Eumenes and allowed him to pass the river. In short, he wanted Eumenes and his strong army out of his satrapy and thus let them continue into Susiana. If the royal troops were indeed Eumenes', as I believe, this means that they cannot have crossed the river before late October. Thus he cannot have been in Susa before November. Eumenes had his troops march in separate columns; since no corn (barley) was available (fitting well with the proposed time of year, since the harvest would have been in April, see chapter 6), rice, sesame and dates were provided as rations during the march.

Seleucus, however, did not passively allow events to unfold. He immediately sent a message to Antigonus, asking him to come as soon as possible, before the satraps and their troops met Eumenes at Susa. As it turned out, the eastern satraps had already gathered at Susa for a meeting due to their fear of Peithon, and Eumenes' couriers found them ready to join him against Peithon and his ally Seleucus. Diodorus Siculus describes the troops of the various satraps and their numbers (XIX.14). Peucestas of Persia had the largest army, described as consisting of 10,000 Persian archers and slingers, 3,000 men of all nationalities equipped to form a Macedonian phalanx and 600 Greek and Thracian horsemen together with 400 Persian horsemen. The army of the satrap Eudamus from India included 500 horse, 300 infantry and 120 elephants, which, according to Diodorus

---

12   Bosworth 2002, 110 describes this episode excellently. According to him, it happened in April/May (317), a time of year when the water level is high.

Fig. 5 | *Tetradrachm minted at Pergamum during the time of Philetaerus. Obverse: Idealized portrait of Seleucus I; Reverse: Seated Athena with spear and shield and the inscription* Philetairou. *The reverse motif is also seen on Lysimachus coins minted at Pergamum. This coin must be minted after 274 (Mørkholm 1991, 128). Though we know from inscriptions that statues – standing or on horseback – of Seleucus were erected during his lifetime, none has so far been identified with certainty, though several have been suggested (see R. Fleischer 1991).*

Siculos, he had acquired after having treacherously killed Porus.[13] Euda-mus received money from Eumenes for feed for the elephants, while the other satraps paid for their own forces.

Antigonus wintered in Mesopotamia in 317/316. He had set out from Cilicia in pursuit of Eumenes with an army of 20,000 lightly equipped infantry and 4,000 cavalry (Diod. Sic. XVIII.73.1) – a force about the same size as Eumenes' – and planned to follow him as soon as his own army was ready. Thus he may actually have been close to Eumenes and the royal army, who were in Babylonia. According to Diodorus, Antigonus at first planned to follow Eumenes closely before increasing his own strength.

---

13 Peithon, who had been appointed by Alexander as satrap of 'the land extending from the confluence of the Indus and Acesines as far as the sea, together with all the coastland of India' (Arr. *Anab.* VIb) in 325, is not listed by Diodorus Siculus; he appears only in 316 or 315 (depending on chronology), coming to Babylon to be appointed satrap of Babylonia by Antigonus.

When he learned that Eumenes had already met the eastern satraps, he slowed his speed in order to refresh his troops and enroll more soldiers, realising 'that the war called for large armies and for no ordinary preparation' (Diod. Sic. XIX.15.6). If Diodorus Siculus is correct, Antigonus can have learnt this only in November, when Seleucus and Peithon realised that Eumenes had met the eastern satraps.

After these preparations, Antigonus came to Babylonia and agreed a joint action against Eumenes with Seleucus and Peithon. He was allocated soldiers by both, had a pontoon bridge established across the Tigris and crossed with his army. Antigonus entered Susa with his army, together with Seleucus and Peithon. Here, Seleucus was appointed satrap also of Susiana instead of Antigenes, and asked to lay siege to the citadel, since Xenophilus had refused to accept Antigonus' orders. Antigonus probably left Seleucus behind for two reasons: he may have trusted Seleucus more and he wanted to keep Peithon and his army closer at hand. Like Seleucus, Peithon also knew the region well and had proven himself a very good leader, but also very ambitious.

Antigonus' campaign against Eumenes in Iran turned out to be one of the great campaigns during the period of the Diadochs (Diod. Sic. XIX.17). The outcome was uncertain, but in the end Antigonus won the final victory. While still in Iran, the talent and ambitions of Peithon made Antigonus suspicious, and he had him executed and a new satrap of Media appointed. From the treasury of Ecbatana, Antigonus brought 5,000 talents of uncoined silver and continued to Persepolis. Now considering himself Lord of Asia he continued to Susa, taking up residence at the citadel. By this time Seleucus had probably gone back to Babylonia.

Having appointed Aspisas satrap of Susiana, thus depriving Seleucus of his double position, Antigonus prepared wagons and camels, and set out to return to the west with his army and an enormous treasure. His victorious anabasis had eliminated Eumenes and Peithon, and he was now in a position to challenge his rivals in the west. Antigonus arrived in Babylon after a march of 22 days from Susa. According to BCHP 3 line 38, he was in Babylon from 25 June until 24 July; according to the low chronology, this must have been in 315. Seleucus met him there, with gifts suitable for a king, and held feasts for the whole army. However, the situation soon became confrontational, when Seleucus denied Antigonus the right to see the satrapal accounts, and thereby clearly challenged Antigonus' right to overall authority. According to Diodorus, he protested that he had been given the satrapy by the Macedonians in recognition of 'his services rendered while Alexander was still alive' (XIX.55.4). According to Appian (Syr. 53), Seleucus had punished one of the governors without consulting

Antigonus, who was present, and the latter became angry, demanding an account of Seleucus' money and possessions.

He had, however, seen what had happened to Peithon, seen Peucestas removed from power and personally experienced replacement in Susiana by Aspisas; realistically he knew that he would not stand a chance against Antigonus. Accordingly, he decided to escape to Egypt with 50 horsemen. He must have been confident of receiving support from Ptolemy, or, at least, of his own ability to induce Ptolemy to become seriously concerned regarding the intentions of Antigonus (Diod. Sic. XIX.55). Antigonus was at first very pleased to see the back of Seleucus, but he soon began to worry when Chaldean astrologers came to him and foretold that, if he let Seleucus escape, Seleucus would become master of all Asia (Diod. Sic. XXI, Dindorf fr. 3). Whether in response to this prophecy or simply due to second thoughts, Antigonus decided to send out men to pursue Seleucus. However, they had to give up the pursuit and return to the city.

CHAPTER 4

The years in the Mediterranean and the return to Babylonia

Arriving safely in Egypt, Seleucus was met with kindness (*philanthropia*) by Ptolemy, according to Diodorus Siculus (XIX.56). Seleucus accused Antigonus of wanting to deprive all men of rank, and 'in particular those who had served under Alexander',[1] of their satrapies. He noted the removal of Peucestas from Persis, the execution of Peithon and his own experiences; 'all these men, who were guiltless of wrongdoing and had even performed great services out of friendship, had been patiently awaiting a reward for virtue'. He also stressed the threatening size of Antigonus' army, his vast wealth and his recent successes, and that this had made him arrogant, nourishing hopes of becoming king of 'the whole kingdom of the Macedonians'.

Seleucus succeeded in prompting Ptolemy to prepare for war, and he himself sent some of his friends to Europe in order to convert both Cassander and Lysimachus to side against Antigonus. 'They quickly carried out their instructions, and the seed of a quarrel and of great wars began to grow' (Diod. Sic. XIX.56.3). Seleucus was clearly the driving force in efforts to establish a coalition against Antigonus. He must have held significant prestige and trustworthiness among the other satraps, since by now he actually had no power other than his military talent. In contrast to Antigonus, he had, like Ptolemy and Lysimachus, campaigned with Alexander all the way to India and stayed in Babylon at the time of his death. He may also have been acquainted with Cassander, son of Antipater, who had come to Babylon in 323; at Triparadeisus he was the one who, together with Antigonus, had prevented the quarrel between the Macedonian army and Antipater from escalating further (see chapter 2). Ptolemy and Lysimachus had also

---

[1]   At this time, soldiers of any rank who had participated in Alexander's eastern campaign clearly saw themselves as something special.

known Peithon well, all three being members of Alexander's Bodyguard. But more than any of these reasons, the simple fact that Antigonus was now moving west into Cilicia probably convinced the others to join the coalition.

Antigonus, however, foreseeing the plans of Seleucus, also sent envoys to Ptolemy, Lysimachus and Cassander in order to persuade them to maintain their friendship with him. He established Peithon, son of Agenor,[2] who had been appointed satrap of the region 'from the confluence of Akesines and Indus to the sea' by Alexander in 325 (a position confirmed at Babylon and Triparadeisus), as satrap of Babylonia,[3] in place of Seleucus.

In November, Antigonus reached Mallos on the fertile plain of southern Cilicia and divided the army for winter camp. From the treasury at Cyinda he took 10,000 talents and collected the annual revenue of 11,000 talents; altogether this was a formidable sum with which he could sustain his vast army and secure its loyalty. He probably broke winter camp as early as possible in the spring of 315/314 and set out for northern Syria, where envoys from Ptolemy, Lysimachus and Cassander met him. During a meeting of the Macedonian army council (*synedrion*) they demanded that Cappadocia and Lycia be given to Cassander, Hellespontine Phrygia to Lysimachus, all of Syria to Ptolemy and Babylonia to Seleucus. Furthermore, they required Antigonus to share with them the spoils from his victory over Eumenes, since they too had participated in the war. Alternatively, they would all wage war against him. These demands clearly went beyond the agreement reached at Triparadeisus;[4] Lycia, for example, had been assigned to Antigonus already in Babylon and this was confirmed at Triparadeisus. Seleucus had indeed contributed to some extent to Antigonus' victory over Eumenes, but this could hardly be said of the others. Thus, these claims must have sounded, to a man like Antigonus, like a declaration of war, rather than a proposal to be negotiated;[5] and the coalition must have known that their demands would lead to war. Antigonus, now master of the rich satrapies in the east as well as most of Asia Minor and northern Syria, with a large army and enormous wealth, probably did not take the threat seriously. He made it clear that he had no intention of fulfilling these demands and told Ptolemy, Lysimachus and Cassander to prepare themselves for war. These three then made an alliance (Diod. Sic. XIX.57.3).

---

2   See Heckel 1992, 323.
3   He is not included in the list of eastern satraps bringing troops to Eumenes (Diod. Sic. XIX, 14).
4   Waterfield 2011,108 calls the demands an ultimatum.
5   Antigonus seems never to have been a man of compromise and, as Hammond and Walbank 1988, 150 states, 'He preferred war, civil war, to any form of compromise.'

From the experience of his campaign against Eumenes, Antigonus had clearly learnt the necessity of dealing effectively with the enormous scale of Asia. He had a system of fire signals installed across that part of Asia of which he was master and set up a dispatch-carrier system so that messages could very quickly reach all regions; this was undoubtedly a 'revival' of the Achaemenid system (Xen. *Cyr.* XVII–XVIII).[6] He personally moved into Phoenicia in order to organise a fleet, fully aware of the many ships of his opponents in contrast to his own limited maritime resources. Intending to lay siege to Tyre, he camped at Old Tyre, where once Alexander had camped, and asked the kings of Phoenicia and the sub-kings/hyparchs of Syria to join him for a meeting, at which he instructed them to assist in a programme of shipbuilding since all the Phoenician ships and their crews were held in Egypt; Ptolemy had foreseen what was to come and had transferred the Phoenician fleet to Egypt.

While Antigonus was staying at Old Tyre, Seleucus arrived from Egypt with a hundred fine ships (Diod. Sic. XIX.58.5) and sailed past the camp. He thus managed to worry the men from cities allied with Antigonus, because they could clearly foresee that, as long as the ships of Antigonus' opponents ruled the sea, they would be able to plunder their home territories. Seleucus certainly knew how to use psychological warfare. To calm his men, Antigonus promised them that by the summer he would take to the sea with 500 ships.

Later we find Seleucus[7] in a naval operation by besieging Erythrai, an ally of Antigonus. When Seleucus learnt that Antigonus' general Polemaeus was approaching, he broke off the siege and sailed away.

In the meantime, Antigonus conducted a political masterstroke. Together with Alexander, son of Polyperchon, he raised accusations against Cassander in the assembly (*synedrion*) of the Macedonian army and settlers.[8] He accused his opponent of (1) the murder of Olympias and the poor treatment of Roxane and the king, (2) of forcing Thessalonike, a daughter of Philip and half-sister of Alexander, to marry him and so attempting to establish his claim to the Macedonian throne and (3) of refounding Olynthus in his own name (Cassandreia) and rebuilding Thebes, which had been razed by the Macedonians. The assembly voted in favour of a decree

---

6　For a brief discussion of the Achaemenid royal roads, see Meadows 2005; see also Graf 1994.

7　Seleucus is clearly never the main focus of Diodorus (and probably not of Hieronymus either). He is only mentioned in connection with either Antigonus, the main character of the book, or Ptolemy and his troops. We must assume that the hundred ships with which he sailed past Antigonus' camp formed the basis of his activities during this early part of the Third Diadoch War.

8　Diodorus Siculus uses the word *parepidemontoi* (sojourn as a stranger in a place); this is likely to be understood as referring to Macedonians who had settled and were no longer in active service.

stating that Cassander would be considered an enemy unless he destroyed these two cities, released Roxane and the king, and handed them over to the Macedonians (i.e. Antigonus), and accepted Antigonus as general and *epimeletes*. Among Antigonus' promises in return for supporting him were the pledges that all Greeks were to be free and that there should be no foreign garrisons.[9] According to Diodorus Siculus (XIX.61.4), Antigonus assumed that these measures would secure him the Greeks and the satraps and generals of the Upper Satrapies as allies. Messengers were sent out in all directions to announce this.

Alexander was sent back to the Peloponnese with 500 talents to finance war against Cassander. Antigonus himself sailed against Tyre, which now fell after a siege that had lasted no less than a year and three months; the besieged had been brought to a point of extreme want. Antigonus allowed Ptolemy's soldiers who had fought for the city to leave with their possessions; then he installed his own garrison.

When Ptolemy learnt of the decree declaring freedom for all Greeks, he published a similar one. As Diodorus Siculus states (XIX.62.2): 'Each of them, indeed, perceiving that it was a matter of no little moment to gain the goodwill of the Greeks, rivalled the other in conferring favours upon this people.'

Next we find Seleucus having arrived on Cyprus with his fleet and met with Polycleitus, an admiral of Ptolemy. Together they decided that the latter should go to the Peloponnese with 50 ships to fight against Polyperchon and Alexander. It was further agreed that the Athenian commander Myrmidon should go to Caria, where the satrap Asander was being attacked by Antigonus's general Polemaeus. Seleucus and Ptolemy's brother Menelaus should stay on Cyprus to fight together with king Nicocreon, the most powerful of the Cypriot kings, and their other allies. As to the cities on the island who had entered an alliance with Antigonus, Seleucus took Ceryneia and Lapithus, and made an alliance with the king of Marion; he forced Amathus to give a guarantee and laid siege to Cition, a city that he had not succeeded in persuading to join him (Diod. Sic. XIX.62.6).

Later in the year (314 according to the low chronology, 315 according to Diodorus), as Polyperchon and Cassander continued to battle for supreme power over the Peloponnese, Seleucus sent Polycleitus to Kenkraia to offer support to Cassander. However, the situation had changed: Alexander had made an alliance with Cassander. Polycleitus and his force then sailed to Pamphylia and along the coast to Aphrodisias in Cilicia, where

---

9   This had earlier been proclaimed by Polyperchon during the Second Diadoch War.

he won a battle against not only Antigonus' ships but also his land forces. He then continued, via Cyprus, to Pelusium in Egypt. Here he was praised by Ptolemy and bestowed with rich gifts. Ptolemy released some of his high-ranking prisoners after a request to do so from an envoy from Antigonus. The two men actually met at Ecregma on the border between Egypt and Palestine, but Ptolemy went back to Egypt when Antigonus would not accept his demands.

Cassander had been campaigning in western Greece, in Aetolia and Illyria, and on return to Macedonia he learnt that war had been declared by Antigonus against all the cities of Caria, which were allies of Ptolemy and Seleucus (Diod. Sic. XIX, 66). Cassander sent an army to Caria in order both to help his allies and to keep Antigonus from crossing into Europe. He ordered Demetrius of Phaleron and Dionysius, the commander of the garrison at Munichia, to send 20 ships to Lemnos. Aristotle, the commander of these Athenian ships, called in Seleucus and a fleet, and attempted to persuade the Lemnians to revolt against Antigonus. They declined to do so; Lemnos was ravaged and the city besieged. Seleucus, however, sailed off to Cos, a move that gave Dioscurides, Antigonus' admiral, the opportunity to break the siege of Lemnos and capture Aristotle's ships. Diodorus Siculus does not explain why Seleucus left for Cos; in fact, we hear nothing further of him in the narrative until 313, when Antigonus was campaigning in Asia Minor (see below).

Cos was one of the most important of the Aegean islands in the Hellenistic period, with extensive harbour facilities. A very fragmentary inscription from the island honours Nicomedes of Cos (dated 315–307: *Iscrizioni di Cos* ED71; *IG* XII.4). Nicomedes was clearly a high-ranking diplomat at Antigonus' court, who had honours bestowed on him by Athens and several of the Aegean islands. Many eastern Aegean islands were allies of Antigonus.[10] Whether Cos was at this time an ally of Antigonus is not known, but it is probable. If this was the case, Seleucus may have decided to keep up the dynamics of the war instead of staying bogged down in the siege of Lemnos, which he may have thought Aristotle could handle on his own.

Cassander's activities in Asia Minor, though not particularly successful, finally made Antigonus himself act. In autumn 313 he left his 22-year-old son Demetrius in command of Syria with four experienced advisers, among whom were Nearchus and Peithon, satrap of Babylonia, who had accompanied Antigonus to Phoenicia or had been asked to come. He also left about 13,000 infantry men (consisting of 10,000 mercenaries, 2,000 Macedonians,

---

10   Such as Lemnos, Rhodes, Samos and Chios: Billows 1997, 118 n. 45.

Fig. 7 | *Mount Taurus.*

500 Lycians and Pamphylians, and 400 Persian forces), 5,000 cavalry troops and 43 elephants. Antigonus himself, with the rest of the army, attempted to cross the Taurus mountains, but deep snow caused the loss of many soldiers and forced him to return to Cilicia. He used another route to reach Phrygia, where he divided his army for winter camp.

In the summer of 313, Cyrene had revolted against Ptolemy, who had sent an army to suppress the uprising. At this point, he decided it was time he took a direct role in the war, and, with an army, he went personally to Cyprus to fight those kings who opposed him. He defeated his opponents, destroyed Marion (the city with which Seleucus had made an alliance in 314) and had its inhabitants moved to Paphos. Nicocreon was appointed general (*strategos*) of Cyprus, and Ptolemy and his army sailed to Upper Syria, where he conquered and destroyed Poseideion (located between the later cities of Seleucia Pieria and Laodicaea) and Potamoi Charon; these were two of the few cities that had existed in northern Syria during the

Achaemenid period.[11] Afterwards he sailed along the coast to Cilicia where he captured Mallos and sold into slavery the prisoners he had taken. Furthermore, the surrounding country was plundered and the spoils distributed among his army, in order to maintain the soldiers' spirits. He then sailed back to Cyprus.

Ptolemy's mobile warfare led Demetrius to make a fateful decision: he decided to split his army. Leaving behind Peithon with the elephants and heavy-armed units, he moved, with the cavalry and light-armed units, towards Cilicia. Arriving too late, he quickly returned to his camp, but only after losing many horses due to the speed of the march.

Satisfied with his achievements, Ptolemy returned to Egypt. Seleucus' anger towards Antigonus, however, did not die, and Ptolemy himself can hardly have accepted the situation of Demetrius staying on with a large army in Coele Syria, and he therefore gathered his troops to campaign against him. He set out from Alexandria to Pelusium with an army of 18,000 infantry and 4,000 cavalry troops. Diodorus describes this army as including some Macedonians and some mercenaries, and also a large number of Egyptians who were not only used for missile and baggage carrying but also as battle troops.[12] He camped near the enemy at Old Gaza in Syria. Demetrius had also gathered his troops from their winter quarters. The Marmor Parium (*FGrH* 239 B16) dates the battle at Gaza to 312/311; modern scholars normally date it to autumn 312.[13] Demetrius' friends and advisors strongly warned him not to march against a general of Ptolemy's calibre[14] who had a superior force. But Demetrius did not listen, and his youth and charisma made the soldiers enthusiastic supporters of his decision to fight. As Diodorus drily remarks: 'because he had just been placed in command, neither soldiers nor civilians had for him any ill will such as usually develops against generals of long standing when at a particular time many minor irritations are combined in a single mass grievance; for the multitude becomes exacting when it remains under the same authority,

---

11 See Hannestad 2013.
12 Ptolemy had by now created regiments of Egyptians; clearly this was a surprise to Diodorus, who probably reflects Hieronymus' reaction.
13 On the chronological problems of this period, see Wheatley 1998. She argues for the so-called high chronology for the early part of the period and concludes, as do several other scholars, that the battle at Gaza took place in autumn/winter 312. This would mean that Demetrius' army had already camped for winter and was called out again since Ptolemy's invasion of Palestine and Phoenicia came as a surprise. The argument for the battle taking place in autumn depends on numismatics. Ptolemy struck his new type of coin – with Alexander's head wearing an elephant scalp on the obverse and, on the reverse, a fighting Athena – of Attic weight at the mint of Sidon. The coin is dated to year 22 of the Sidonian era, which corresponds to 312/311 (Mørkholm 1991, 65).
14 Here Diodorus (XIX.81) uses the singular, which must refer to Ptolemy.

and every group that is not preferred welcomes change' (XIX.81.3). Demetrius was only too keen to fight against generals 'who were almost the greatest, Ptolemy and Seleucus'. Thus Diodorus adds: 'Indeed, these generals, who had taken part with Alexander in all his wars and had often led armies independently, were unconquered up to the time.'

Demetrius chose the traditional battle formation with about 3,000 cavalry troops on the left wing, where he himself fought together with Peithon. On this wing were also 30 elephants with lightly armed men, including javelin throwers and archers, with 500 Persian slingers interspersed. The central section consisted of a phalanx of 11,000 men, 2,000 of whom were Macedonians, 1,000 Lycians and Pamphylians, and 8,000 mercenaries. In front of them, 13 elephants were stationed with light infantry interspersed. The right wing consisted of 1,500 cavalrymen led by Andronicus. The plan was to hold back the right wing, to await the outcome of Demetrius' fight on the left.

Ptolemy and Seleucus[15] also originally planned to fight on their left wing, but they reversed this decision and decided to fight on the right, opposite Demetrius, after scouts had revealed Demetrius' plans. They also chose 3,000 of their cavalry to fight with them on the right wing. In front they placed men who were to handle the spiked devices made of iron and connected by chains that they had prepared as defence against the elephants, together with their light infantry; they ordered the javelin throwers and slingers to shoot continuously against the elephants and those seated on them.

The initial phase of the battle involved the cavalry fighting first with spears and then swords. As usual in this period, the generals themselves participated actively at the front of the heavy fighting. In the second phase, Demetrius' elephants advanced in order to provoke terror. However, Ptolemy and Seleucus had extensive experience of dealing with war elephants going back to the battle against Porus, and, as Diodorus Siculus states, Ptolemy had cleverly chosen a terrain that was difficult for elephants to negotiate (XIX.84.3–4). The outcome was that all the elephants were captured. This proved too much for Demetrius' horsemen, who took flight. Demetrius himself was left with little support, and he too was forced to flee when the situation fell totally out of control. With his cavalry, he turned back towards Gaza in some kind of order, followed by his disordered infan-

---

15 Diodorus mentions them as equals (XIX.83.1), while Plutarch, in his *Vit. Demtr.* mentions only Ptolemy. Diodorus is, on this point, definitely more trustworthy. But his description of the battle and what happened afterwards also mentions only Ptolemy.

Fig. 8 | *Portrait of Ptolemy.*

try, who, on leaving the lines, had left behind all the heavy weapons. By sunset, when Demetrius was passing Gaza, some of his cavalry broke out of the line to enter the city and carry away their baggage. Total confusion arose when the city gates were opened and panic broke out, when each man tried to save his baggage on pack animals. Ptolemy coming up with his troops saw his chance and attacked. The gates were not closed in time, and Ptolemy captured the city. In this last phase of the battle, Seleucus disappears from Diodorus' narrative. Peithon, who Antigonus had appointed satrap of Babylonia as a replacement for Seleucus, was killed in the battle, together with many high-ranking cavalry officers. According to Diodorus, 500 died in the battle; Plutarch records 5,000 killed and 8,000 taken as prisoners. However, Plutarch's figures would encompass most of Demetrius' army, and thus the record offered by Diodorus is probably more accurate.[16]

Diodorus again mentions both Ptolemy and Seleucus after the battle, in relation to Demetrius' quest for permission to fetch his dead from the

16   See also Walbank 1988, 152.

battlefield in order to bury them. This was granted, and, furthermore, the royal baggage (detailed by Plutarch as Demetrius' tents, his military chest and his whole equipage) was handed over without ransom together with the people of Demetrius' court. According to Diodorus, Ptolemy and Seleucus said, that they had fought with Antigonus against Perdiccas and Eumenes, and that the reason for their disagreement with him was because he had not turned over to his companions their share of the captured territory, and again because he had taken away from Seleucus his satrapy of Babylonia 'contrary to all right' (XIX.85.3). Finally, Ptolemy sent the captured soldiers to Egypt to be distributed among the nomes (provinces) and he organised a magnificent burial for those of his men who had died in battle.

Demetrius retired up the coast to Tripolis, sending a message to Antigonus asking for help. He also began summoning soldiers from Cilicia and from among the troops guarding cities held by Antigonus. Ptolemy, meanwhile, followed up the victory by conquering the southern part of Palestine, briefly. For Seleucus, the battle at Gaza gave him the opportunity he had undoubtedly been waiting for since his escape from Babylon three (low chronology) years earlier. When Seleucus asked Ptolemy for soldiers, the latter readily consented and promised to aid him in every way until he had regained Babylonia (Diod. Sic. XIX.86.5). In fact, Seleucus received no more than eight hundred foot soldiers and about two hundred horses according to Diodorus (XIX.90.1); according to Appian (XI.54), he was allocated 1,000 infantry and 300 cavalry troops. But Seleucus declared that he would have made the expedition into the interior with no army but his friends and his own slaves, counting on the Babylonians to join him immediately since their former relationship had been good, and because Antigonus, by taking his army to Cilicia, had given him an excellent opportunity (Diod. Sic. XIX.90.1). The death of Peithon in the battle at Gaza gave him the further advantage that there was no satrap in Babylonia to oppose him.

Seleucus' friends were, sensibly, less confident when they realised how few men would be campaigning with them. Seleucus, seeing that they were terrified, encouraged them, saying that 'men who had campaigned with Alexander and had been advanced by him because of their prowess ought not to rely solely on armed force and wealth when confronting difficult situations, but upon experience and skill, the means whereby Alexander himself had accomplished his great and universally admired deeds' (Diod. Sic. XIX.90.2).[17] He also told them that, during a consultation, the Oracle at Didyma had addressed him as King Seleucus and that Alexander

---

17 This passage can hardly come from Hieronymus; it must be from one of Diodorus' other sources.

had come to him in his dreams and given him a clear sign of future rule (*hegemonia*) that was destined to fall to him in the course of time. 'Moreover he pointed out that everything that is good and admired among men is gained through toil and danger.' (Diod. Sic. XIX.90.5). Seleucus' visit to Didyma is sometimes assumed to have taken place when Alexander visited the sanctuary in 334 in connection with his conquest of the city.[18] However, it is more likely that Seleucus visited the Oracle a second time in relation to his command of part of Ptolemy's fleet before Antigonus later 'liberated' the city. 'But he also sought the favour of his fellow soldiers and put himself on an equality with them in such a way that each man respected him and willingly accepted the risk of the daring venture' (Diod. Sic. XIX.90).

The route[19] he chose from Gaza (or possibly from Tyre, if he marched together with Ptolemy and his army) was probably up to Damascus (since Demetrius was at Tripolis) and then onwards via Homs, Hama and Aleppo in order to cross the Euphrates and the Tigris, following the royal road.[20] When Seleucus had crossed the Euphrates, settlers at Carrhae were persuaded or forced to join him. When he entered Babylonia, 'most of the inhabitants came to meet him, and, declaring themselves on his side, promised to aid him as he saw fit; for, when he had been for four years satrap of that country, he had shown himself generous to all, winning the goodwill (*eunoia*) of the common people, and long in advance securing men who would assist him if an opportunity should ever be given him to make a bid for supreme power' (Diod. Sic. XIX.91.1–2).[21] Furthermore, Polyarchus, who had been in command of a particular district (*dioikesis*) and who had more than 1,000 soldiers joined him. Supporters of Antigonus, clearly a minority, took refuge in one of the two citadels of Babylon. Seleucus lay siege to the citadels, took them by storm and freed his friends and slaves, who had been held there ever since Seleucus' escape from the city. He enlisted soldiers and bought horses, which he distributed among those of his men who had experience in riding. 'Associating with all on friendly terms and raising high hopes in all, he kept his fellow adventurers ready and eager under every condition. In this way, then, Seleucus regained Babylonia' (Diod. Sic. XIX.91.5).

---

18 App. *Syr.* 56 tells of another omen that Seleucus received when visiting Didyma with Alexander. In this instance, the Oracle had told him not to hurry back to Europe; Asia would be much better for him.

19 See Engels 1978, 64–70 for a discussion of the routes Alexander may have taken from Tyre when following the Persian king.

20 See Briant 2002, fig. 35.

21 Here it is obvious that Diodorus has used sources other than Hieronymus.

According to the *Babylonian Chronicle* BCHP 3, reverse column 4 line 3, Seleucus declared sometime after the end of May that: 'year 7 of Antigonus the general you will from now on count as year 6 of Alexander, son of Alexander and Seleucus the general'. By making this announcement he clearly made the claim that he was now master of Babylonia.[22]

In Media, general Nicanor[23] gathered more than 10,000 infantry soldiers and about 7,000 cavalry from Media and Persis (reflecting the wealth of horses in Media) (Diod. Sic. XIX.92). However, when Seleucus heard of this, he reacted promptly and set out against the enemy at full speed, though with an army of no more than 3,000 infantry and 400 horsemen. He crossed the Tigris, and, on learning that his opponent was only a few days' march away, he hid his soldiers in the swamps close to the river and waited for an opportunity to mount a surprise attack. Nicanor fell into Seleucus' trap. Upon arriving at the Tigris, since there was no trace of the enemy, he stopped at one of the royal camps (*stathmoi*), assuming that Seleucus was some distance away. As planned, Seleucus took Nicanor by surprise – by a dawn attack, we may assume – and created panic and confusion. The commander (here called 'satrap' by Diodorus) of the Persians, Euager, was killed[24] together with other commanders (*hegemones*). Consequently, most of the soldiers joined Seleucus, partly out of fear but also because they were offended by Antigonus' behaviour. Nicanor and a few men escaped through the desert, 'but Seleucus, now that he had gained control of a large army and was comporting himself in a way gracious to all, easily won over Susiana, Media, and some of the adjacent lands; and he wrote to Ptolemy and his other friends about his achievements, already possessing a king's stature and a reputation worthy of royal power' (Diod. Sic. XIX.92.5).

---

22 Actually year 311 became the first year of the so-called Seleucid Era (S.E.). In contrast to the ordinary practice in Hellenistic times of counting time by each king, Antiochus I adopted what must be seen as a more ambitious dynastic system that also honoured his father. The system was based precisely on Seleucus' return to Babylon in 311, which was counted as the first year of the Seleucid Era (S.E.). A tablet written in late Babylonian script from the late second century, now in the British Museum (B.M. 35603), illustrates the system. 'Year 7 [of S.E., i.e. Seleucid Era] = 305–304, which is [his] first year, Seleucus [ruled] as king. He reigned 25 years. 'Year 31(SE.) he was killed in the land [of the] Khani. Year 32 [S.E.], An[tiochus] the son of Se[leucus ruled as] king. He reigned 20 Years. Year 51 [SE. month] II, [day] 16, An[tiochus] the great king died.' Antiochus died on 1 June 261 BC (Sachs and Wiseman 1954, see also Boiy 2000 and van der Spek https://www.livius.org/sources/content/mesopotamian-chron-icles-content/babylonian-king-list-of-the-hellenistic-period/). The system was still in use in areas of the former Seleucid kingdom in the sixth century AD, and even later. See Kosmin 2018.

23 Not Hippostratus, whom Antigonus had appointed general four years earlier (see chapter 3). We hear nothing of the local Orontobates (see chapter 3) who had been appointed satrap after Peithon.

24 Geer 1954 suggests that this could be the Euagoras who is mentioned earlier as satrap of Aria.

When news of these events reached Antigonus (Diod. Sic. XIX.100.2ff), he decided to send Demetrius east with an army of 5,000 Macedonians and 10,000 mercenaries, together with 4,000 cavalry troops. Demetrius was ordered to recapture Babylon together with the satrapy and then to return to the Mediterranean. When Patrocles, whom Seleucus had appointed general of Babylonia, learnt that Demetrius had set out from Damascus, he employed his knowledge of the topography and climate of Babylonia in a masterly way. He ordered the civilians to leave the city; some of them were to cross the Euphrates and take refuge in the desert while others were ordered to go to Susiana or down to the coast of the Gulf. Patrocles and his men also left the city and, once in the countryside, they used the rivers and canals of the region to conduct a kind of guerilla warfare. Patrocles, of course, sent a message to Seleucus, who was by this time in Media, asking him to come as soon as possible. Demetrius arrived in Babylon and found the city empty apart from the two citadels, which he besieged. One of the citadels was quickly taken and, as a reward, it was handed to his soldiers to be looted. The other citadel proved more of a challenge, and after a few days he left it to one of his friends, Archelaus, to maintain the siege, leaving him with 5,000 infantry and 1,000 horsemen, while he himself marched back with the remainder of his army to Syria. He also also allowed his soldiers to plunder the country for their own use, and then return to the sea (the Mediterranean). Plutarch (*Vit. Demtr.* VII.2) considered this to be an advantage of Seleucus 'for his (Demetrius') laying waste the country seemed as if he had no farther claim to it'[25]

In the west, after Ptolemy's attempt to conquer Palestine, a treaty was entered into between Cassander, Ptolemy and Lysimachus, on one side, and Antigonus on the other. Antigonus reports on the treaty, and his reasons for entering into it are preserved on an inscription in Scepsis in Troas with a letter dated to 311. Central to the letter is Antigonus stressing his eagerness to protect the freedom of the Greeks.[26]

'We have written a clause into the agreement that all the Greeks should join together in protecting their mutual freedom and autonomy, in the belief that in our lifetime they would in all human expectation be preserved, but that in future with all the Greeks and the men in power bound by oath, the freedom of the Greeks would be much more securely guaranteed. To join in the oath to protect what we agreed with each other did not seem inglorious or without advantage to the Greeks.

---

25 Translation J. and W. Langhorne, www.attalus.or/old/demetriusl.html.
26 The letter was undoubtedly sent to many Greek cities in Asia Minor and the Islands.

It therefore seems to me right that you should swear the oath which we have sent to you. We shall endeavour in future to achieve whatever is in your interests and that of other Greeks.' [27]

The treaty may reflect a need for peace and stability that they all felt was essential, by this time, in order to consolidate their empires. Cassander was to be general in Europe until Roxane's son, Alexander, came of age; Lysimachus would be master of Thrace; Ptolemy would be master of Egypt and cities in Libya and Arabia, while Antigonus would be master of the whole of Asia; and the Greeks were to be free. The treaty thus clearly did not include a position for Seleucus on the same level as those offered to Lysimachus, Cassander and Ptolemy. That Antigonus was to be master of all Asia can only have meant that Seleucus was expected to accept Antigonus as his master. Clearly, neither Lysimachus, Ptolemy nor Cassander saw Seleucus as their equal at this point in time. Seleucus' aim had always been to be re-established as satrap of Babylonia, and Ptolemy had given him his support, for which Seleucus had paid. Ptolemy and Lysimachus had been members of Alexander's Bodyguard and Cassander was the son of Antipater. Though Ptolemy and Seleucus were probably close already during their years serving with Alexander, their backgrounds and social standings were very different.

The treaty shows that, 12 years after the death of Alexander, reference to 'the kings' or 'the king' as the absolute centre of power was no longer relevant. The king had been reduced to ruling over Macedonia alone.[28] Accordingly, Antigonus no longer needed the title of *epimeletes*, and, at the time of the treaty, his power was at its absolute zenith. None of the four men, however, respected the treaty; instead, they manoeuvred independently for more power. Cassander secretly had Roxane and her son killed and buried the very same year, and so the impression that there was still a king of Macedonia was finally stripped away. For Cassander, of course, this eliminated the threat to his power in Macedonia, and, according to Diodorus, it relieved all four men of 'their anticipated danger from the king; for henceforth, there being no longer anyone to inherit the realm, each of those who had rule over nations or cities entertained hopes of royal power and held the territory that had been placed under his authority as if it were a kingdom won by the spear' (XIX.105.4).[29] A new order had finally

---

27 Translation Austin 2006, no. 31.
28 For a different opinion, see Hammond 1988, 162.
29 Polyperchon had Barsine and Heracles (possibly a pretender, not a son of Barsine) brought from Pergamum during his conflict with Cassander, who, however, persuaded Polyperchon to have Heracles killed (Diod. Sic. XX.20.1–2).

started to emerge, and it would take only a few more years to formalise it, when these men all anointed themselves as kings.

With Demetrius' departure from Babylon, Seleucus again disappears from our Greco-Roman literary sources. Among the fragments of the *Babylonian Chronicles*, however, is an account of what was apparently a campaign launched by Antigonus against Seleucus in 210 after the defeat of Nicanor and the return of Demetrius. Strangely, Diodorus passes over this incident completely. The very fragmentary narrative (BCHP 3 part 2) has given a name to the 'Babylonian War'.[30] 'In year 7 [310/309] month Abu [17 August to 15 September 310] of Alexander, the king, son of Alexander, and [Seleucus?]' (lines 14–15 on the reverse of BCHP 3), the scribe states 'that Antigonus [did] battle with the troops of Se[leucus]'. Wheatley (1998) assumes that Antigonus entered Babylonia during the campaigning season of 310, probably within six months of ratifying the peace treaty of 311 with Ptolemy, Lysimachus and Cassander. In the following lines we follow Antigonus, who seems to have plundered the city and the countryside, and, as the text records, 'there was weeping and mourning in the land'. 'In year 8 of Alexander, the king, son of Alexander, and of Seleucus the General [309/308], Archelaus and the troops of Antigonus did battle with the troops of Seleucus in early August' (BCHP 3 left edge lines 1–2). The *Astronomical Diaries* of the period also note Antigonus fighting in the city (*AD* I, pp. 230–1) and a lack of barley on the market.[31]

One of the stratagems presented by Polyaenus (4.9) may relate to the Babylonian War, though this is very uncertain: 'A pitched battle between Seleucus and Antigonus was undecided. When night came, it seemed best to both sides to postpone the fighting until the next day. Antigonus' men encamped unarmed, while Seleucus ordered his soldiers to eat wearing their armor and to sleep in battle order. Just before daybreak, Seleucus' men advanced armed and in formation. Antigonus' men, caught without arms and in disorder, quickly gave the victory to the enemy'.[32]

While Antigonus was campaigning in Babylonia, Ptolemy renewed hostilities in the Aegean under the pretext that Antigonus had garrisoned some of the Greek cities that the treaty had agreed should be free. Antigonus' younger son, Philip, was sent to the Hellespont to suppress a revolt prompted by Antigonus' general Polemaeus, who was disappointed not to have received more honours after his successful campaign in Asia Minor.

---

30 See Wheatley 2002.
31 See chapter 6.
32 Translation http://www.attalus.org/translate/polyaenus4B.html.

Demetrius fought in Cilicia and defeated Ptolemy's generals who had won some of the cities there. Wars also characterised Greece and the Black Sea area, and on Cyprus Ptolemy's old ally King Nicocles of Paphos seems to have entered into an alliance with Antigonus. However, Ptolemy was quick to realise the danger of a revolt on Cyprus, and had him killed.

By 307, the situation in Greece had become intolerable for Antigonus, who sent Demetrius to restore control over Athens and Megara with the instruction, according to Diodorus Siculus (XX.45), to free all Greek cities; first and foremost among these was Athens, where Cassander had a garrison. Demetrius successfully completed this mission, and Demetrius of Phaleron, Cassander's military governor, escaped to Ptolemy in Egypt.[33] A revolt in Epirus further weakened Cassander's position. In the north, meanwhile, Lysimachus had founded Lysimachaea in 309, but had been mainly kept busy fighting the Thracians.

After Demetrius' success in Athens, Antigonus ordered him to sail against Cyprus and Ptolemy's generals as quickly as possible. He asked the Rhodians for support, but they refused as they intended to remain neutral in the forthcoming conflict.

In spring 306, Demetrius won a complete victory over Ptolemy's forces in a naval battle at Salamis on Cyprus, which resulted in all the cities of the island being in Antigonus' hands. He now decided that the time had come to take the ultimate step and crown himself with the diadem; and 'from that time on he used the style of king; and he permitted Demetrius also to assume this same title and rank' (Diod. Sic. XX.53.2). According to Diodorus, Antigonus was, at the time of the battle at Salamis, staying in upper Syria, where a new city, Antigoneia, was being built on the Orontes river. 'He laid it out on a lavish scale, making its perimeter seventy stades; for the location was naturally well adapted for watching over Babylon and the Upper Satrapies, and again for keeping an eye upon lower Syria and affairs in Egypt' (Diod. Sic.XX.47.5). Antigonus followed up the victory by setting out for Gaza in late October 306 with an army of 8,000 cavalry, 80,000 infantry and 83 elephants, while Demetrius followed along the coast with 150 warships and 100 transporters, despite the pilots' forecast of

---

33 Diod. Sic. book XX.46.1–3 details all the honours that the Athenians awarded Demetrius and Antigonus, as well as Antigonus' benefits. The Athenians voted to set up golden statues of Antigonus and Demetrius in a chariot near the statues of Harmodius and Aristogeiton; to give them both honorary crowns at a cost of 200 talents; to consecrate an altar to them and call it the altar of the saviours; to add two more to the ten tribes, Demetrias and Antigonis; to hold annual games in their honour, with a procession and a sacrifice; and to weave their portraits in the peplos of Athena. An embassy went to Antigonus to deliver the honorary decree and also to discuss what the city needed: grain and timber for ships. Antigonus promised 150,000 *medimnoi* of grain and enough timber for a hundred ships.

bad weather at the setting of the Pleiades (about 1 November) (Diod. Sic. XX.73.3). The forecast proved correct, and much of the fleet was wrecked on the harbourless coast. Furthermore, Ptolemy's defensive line along the Nile proved too strong, and Antigonus' supplies began to fail. With the approval of his officers, he decided to retire to Gaza.[34]

Ptolemy celebrated his good luck with sacrifices to the gods and lavish entertainment for his friends. He also wrote to Seleucus, Lysimachus and Cassander about his successes and about the large number of men who had deserted to him (Diod. Sic. XX76.7). This must be the point at which Ptolemy, signaling to Antigonus that he did not recognise him as his superior, proclaimed himself king.[35] Diodorus adds that the rest of the dynasts also called themselves kings out of rivalry: 'Seleucus, who had recently gained the Upper Satrapies, and Lysimachus and Cassander, who still retained the territories originally allotted to them' (XX.53).

It must have been Seleucus' victories in the east (Diod. Sic. XX.53; see also below) that now made him an equal in the eyes of Ptolemy. This brief mention of what Seleucus had achieved since the end of the Babylonian War is characteristic of Diodorus Siculus (and probably Hieronymus) regarding affairs beyond the core regions and main characters of what must have been Hieronymus' narrative of the events of these years. As to chronology, we are left with estimations only.

After the end of the Babylonian War, Seleucus must have spent time in Babylonia in order to settle the country, which had been 'weeping and mourning'(see chapter 6), and he can hardly have been ready to leave Babylonia before 308 or more likely 307,[36] a time that fits well with Antigonus being occupied in the west with war against Cassander and Ptolemy. The *Babylonian Chronicles*, with their focus on Babylon and the surrounding area, tell us nothing about the situation in Media, Susiana and Persis during the Babylonian War. We may assume that Seleucus managed to keep the western Iranian satrapies under his control, and he must, on his way east, have made stops of some length in the Iranian satrapies in order to raise an adequate army and secure his control of these areas. Bactria must

---

34 The campaign is described in detail by Diodorus (XX.35) from the point of view of Antigonus; the passages are clearly taken more or less directly from Hieronymus. Such detail is completely lacking when it comes to the records of the campaigns of Ptolemy and Seleucus.

35 The Parian Marble dates Ptolemy's proclamation of himself as king to the year 305/304 (FGrH 239 B23), while Diodorus Siculus mentions it under the year 306. This is a tendency seen quite often in Diodorus' narrative: he continues a story under a specific year, though it actually took place later (or earlier).

36 I here follow the chronology for the end of the Babylonian War in August 309 (Wheatley 2002), based on studies of BCHP 3 by Finkel and van der Spek (https://www.livius.org/sources/content/mesopotamian-chronicles-content/bchp-3-diadochi-chronicle) and Boiy 2007.

have been his next goal. Whether he fought against the satrap (Stasanor of Soloi), appointed by Antipater at Triparadeisus in 320 and reappointed by Antigonus at Persepolis in 315, low chronology), or against a revolt we do not know. Seleucus knew both Bactria and India from Alexander's campaign. Thus he must have known the terrain, the climate and the peoples well.

Quite a long period must have been spent in Bactria, and Seleucus probably did not reach India until 305/304, an estimation with which other scholars agree.[37] That Seleucus crossed the Indus is highly probable; Alexander had given the region east of the Indus to Peithon, who had fought with Demetrius at Gaza and been killed. What Seleucus may not have known was that, in the meantime, Chandragupta Maurya (in Greek sources Sandrocottus) had conquered the region on the other side of the Indus and set himself up as king or emperor, apparently inspired by Alexander, and that, in this ruler, Seleucus would meet a general of a calibre matching his own. The literary sources concerned with Seleucus during these years are scarce, and the precise date of his campaign in the east is not known. Among the sparse information we have from the Greco-Roman literary sources is Justin's epitome of Pompeius Trogus' *Philippic History* XV.4.

'After the division of the Macedonian empire among the followers of Alexander, he carried on several wars in the east. He first took Babylon, and then, his strength being increased by this success, subdued the Bactrians. He next made an expedition into India, which after the death of Alexander had shaken, as it were, the yoke of servitude from its neck, and put his governors to death. The author of this liberation was Sandrocottus, who afterwards, however, turned their semblance of liberty into slavery; for, making himself king, he oppressed the people whom he had delivered from a foreign power, with cruel tyranny. This man … Sandrocottos, having thus acquired a throne, was in possession of India, when Seleucus was laying the foundations of his future greatness; who after making a league with him, and settling his affairs in the east, proceeded to join in the war against Antigonus.'

Appian (*Syr.* 55) states that Seleucus conquered the east as far as the Indus river, and also that he crossed the Indus and made war with king Sandrocottus 'until they came to an understanding with each other and contracted a marriage relationship – if so, probably a daughter of Seleucus to a son of Sandracottus (see also Strabo 15.2.9). Some of these deeds were

---

37 See Kosmin 2014, 32 with further references.

performed before the death of Antigonus and some afterward'.[38] The agreement between Seleucus and Sandrocottus is also mentioned by Plutarch (*Vit. Alex.*VI.62, where he mentions the 500 elephants given to Seleucus).

Most scholars argue that Seleucus must have lost one or more battles against Sandrocottus, since he rendered over to him the easternmost satrapies of Alexander's empire. However, the fact that the agreement included a gift to Seleucus of a large number of elephants rather suggests a stalemate. Seleucus must have been realistic enough to acknowledge that it would be impossible to keep the easternmost provinces under control in these circumstances. No source gives precise geographical details regarding exactly how much of Alexander's territory Seleucus gave up. Certainly the territories east of the Indus, but, according to Strabo (15.2.9), while 'Alexander took away from the Arians and established settlements of his own … Seleucus Nicator gave up territories west of the Indus which had been part of Alexander's empire and colonized by him to Sandrocottus in consequence of a marriage contract, and received in return five hundred elephants.'[39] As noted above, whilst it is often assumed that Seleucus was defeated in one (or more) battles against Sandrocottus, Kosmin (2014, chapter I) too suggests that it is much more likely that Seleucus, realist as he was, saw that this was a territory that it would be impossible to keep, and that a treaty with Sandrocottus and an exchange of gifts would free him from what would be an impossible task. Kosmin's interesting reflections on the importance of a border support the conclusion that this was certainly something that Seleucus would have agreed to. He thus also gave up Arachosia and Gedrosia or at least parts of these Achaemenid satrapies.[40]

When Seleucus returned to Babylon we do not know. He must have made stops during the long journey back, probably in Persepolis and Susa. According to a cuneiform tablet from Babylon in the British Museum (BM 35603), Seleucus' first year as king was year 7 (305–304).[41] The first coins with his name and the royal title celebrate his Indian campaign.[42]

---

38 Regarding Seleucus' Indian campaign and the treaty entered into with Sandrocottus, Kosmin 2014, chapter I presents a thorough discussion and an interesting, and in my view highly probable, interpretation of the results of Seleucus' campaign.

39 Translation H. L. Jones (Loeb classical Library 1917–32), http://penelope.uchicago.edu/Thayer/E/Roman/Texts/Strabo/home.html

40 See Kosmin 2014, 33 for a recent estimation of the areas that Seleucus did or may have given up.

41 See Sachs and Wiseman 1954; 'Babylonian king list of the Hellenistic period' by R.J. van der Spek (https://www.livius.org/) line 6: Year 7 (SE = 305–304, which is year 1): 'Seleucus [I Nicator was] king'; see also Boiy 2011.

42 Houghton and Lorber 2002, 3.

In Diodorus Siculus' narrative, Seleucus reappears in 302, when Cassander found his situation so alarming that he attempted to make a deal with Antigonus. Antigonus declined, asking instead for Cassander's surrender. Cassander then asked Lysimachus to join him in the inevitable forthcoming confrontation. Together, the two kings sent envoys to 'Ptolemy, king, and to Seleucus, who was ruler (*kyrios*) of the Upper Satrapies' (Diod. Sic. XX.106.2). Ptolemy and Seleucus were apparently easily persuaded to join forces with them. Cassander sent a general with part of his army to Lysimachus and moved into Thessaly to fight Demetrius, while Lysimachus crossed to Asia.

According to Diodorus (XX.108.1), Antigonus was at this time (302) staying in his newly founded capital, Antigoneia, and making large-scale preparations for games and a festival, having gathered together the most famous athletes and artists to compete for expensive prizes and high payouts. When he learnt of Lysimachus' campaign in Asia, he stopped the preparations, paying the athletes and artists no less than 200 talents as compensation. He gathered his army and quickly set out for Tarsus, where he awarded the soldiers three months' pay in advance from money acquired from the treasury at Cyinda, from where Antigonus, in 315, had fetched 10,000 talents (cf. Diod. Sic. XIX.56.4; see chapter 3). He carried 3,000 talents with the army and crossed the Taurus into Cappadocia; he travelled further on into upper Phrygia and Lycaonia, where he managed to restore 'those who had deserted him' to the former alliance. When learning of the advance of Antigonus, Lysimachus held a council at which it was decided not to engage in battle until Seleucus arrived, but rather to use a defensive strategy; the camp was therefore fortified with palisades and a ditch.

When Antigonus arrived, he challenged Lysimachus to battle, but without success; instead, he occupied locations through which Lysimachus had to get his provisions. Lysimachus realised his precarious position and, accordingly, he broke camp at night and at high speed marched 400 stades (c. 80 km) to Doryleion (Eskeşehir), a city with rich supplies of grain and other provisions. The army camped outside the city, where it was protected by a river, and the area was further strengthened with a deep ditch and a triple palisade.

Antigonus then besieged the camp, after sending for catapults and missiles. Lysimachus quickly realised that a shortage of food would soon become a major problem, and therefore decided to break camp. He waited for a stormy night to carry out the manoeuvre, intending to move the army up to the highlands for the winter. At daybreak, Antigonus started to pursue Lysimachus, but moved parallel to him in the lowlands. This choice, however, meant the pursuit was hampered by heavy rain and masses of mud. As a consequence, the pack animals started to die and the men too. In the end, Antigonus was forced to break off the pursuit and move into winter quarters, distributing the army to the best locations available. Thus the campaign season of 302 came to an end.

When Antigonus learnt that Seleucus was coming down from the Upper Satrapies with a large force, he sent some of his supporters to Demetrius in Greece, bidding him to join his father and bring his army 'for, since all the kings had united against him, he was taking every precaution not to be forced to decide the whole battle before the army in Europe came to join him' (Diod. Sic. XX.109.5). In the meantime, Lysimachus' army was by now in winter quarters on the Salonia plain and obtaining ample supplies from Heraclea. This was possible since the very same year he had married Amastris, a niece of Darius who had been married formerly to Craterus. After her divorce from Craterus, she had married Dionysius of Heraclaea in 322 and now ruled the city following his death (Diod. Sic. XVIII.18.7).

And so ends Diodorus' book XX, and with it the continuous narrative, leaving us without the climax of the final battles of the period of the Diadochs. Fragments of book XXI (paraphrases and transcripts from much later) offer us some information. Thus fragment XXI.2[43] briefly states that 'Ptolemy, Seleucus and Lysimachus united against King Antigonus; not so much prompted by goodwill towards one another as compelled by the fears each had for himself, they moved readily to make common cause in the supreme struggle. In the battle, the elephants of Antigonus and Lysimachus fought as if nature had matched them equally in courage and strength.' Fragment XXI.4 records that 'Antigonus, king of Asia, made war against a coalition of four kings, Ptolemy, son of Lagus, king of Egypt, Seleucus, king of Babylonia, Lysimachus, king of Thrace, and Cassander, son of Antipater, king of Macedonia. When he engaged them in battle, he was pierced by many missiles, and his body was carried from the field and was buried with royal honours.'

Plutarch (*Vit.Demtr.* XXVIII) takes up the thread left by Diodorus at the end of his book XX. According to him, Antigonus had an army of 70,000 foot soldiers, 10,000 horses and 75 elephants. Lysimachus and Seleucus could muster 64,000 infantry, 10,500 horses and no less than 400 elephants and 120 armed chariots.[44] Plutarch's description of the Battle of Ipsos is short:

'When the battle was begun, Demetrius, at the head of his best cavalry, fell upon Antiochus, the son of Seleucus, and fought with so much bravery that he put the enemy to flight; but by a vain and unseasonable ambition to go upon the pursuit, he lost the victory; for he went so far that he could not get back to join his infantry, the enemy's elephants having taken up the intermediate space. Seleucus, now seeing his adversary's foot deprived of their horse, did not attack them, but rode around them as if he was going every moment to charge; intending by this manoeuvre both to terrify them and to give them the opportunity to change sides. The event answered his expectation. A large part separated from the main body and voluntarily came over to him; the rest was put to rout.'

Antigonus himself died on the battlefield, pierced by arrows and looking in vain for his son coming to his aid.

---

43 Translation Loeb Diod. Sic. XXI,2. http://penelope.uchicago.edu/Thayer/E/Roman/Texts/Diodorus_Siculus/21*.html.

44 At Gaugamela, Darius had a hundred armed vehicles according to Arrian (III,11,6).

CHAPTER 5

Seleucus' co-regency with his son, victory over Lysimachus and death

At the battle at Ipsus, Seleucus, who was born in either 358 or 354, was in his middle 50s. He would now have another 20 years before he and Lysimachus met as opponents on the battlefield and the time of the Diadochs came to an end.

After the defeat at Ipsus and his father's death (Diod. Sic. XXI.1.4b), Demetrius joined his mother, Stratonice, who had remained in Cilicia with all their valuables, and from there sailed to Cyprus, which was still in his possession. Plutarch's account (*Vit.Demtr.*) is more detailed and differs on some points. Thus, according to him, Demetrius fled from the battlefield with 5,000 infantry and 4,000 cavalry, and soon reached Ephesus. The inhabitants feared that he would plunder the temple to raise money, but he hurried on and sailed to Greece, hoping to be welcomed by the Athenians. They, however, were not interested, and had moved his wife, Daidamaea, from Athens to Megara. Demetrius had also left ships and money in Athens; the Athenians released these to him and Demetrius sailed to the Isthmen, but also here he won no sympathy. The cities had expelled his garrisons and many of the soldiers had defected to his enemies. He then sailed to Chersonesus in order to plunder territory belonging to Lysimachus.

The outcome of the battle at Ipsus was that Lysimachus obtained Lydia, Ionia, Phrygia and the northern coastal area of Asia Minor (i.e. Asia Minor to the Taurus mountains), though a number of Greek cities were more or less free. Pleistarchus, Cassander's brother who had fought with Lysimachus, received Cilicia as reward for his participation in the alliance against Antigonus, though his mission had partly failed (Plut. *Vit.Demtr.* XXXI). According to the agreement reached between Cassander, Lysimachus and Seleucus, Seleucus' share of Antigonus' lands was to encompass Syria, Phoenicia and Palestine, but this proposal led to a confrontation with Ptolemy. Diodorus (XXI.1.4 = fragment 5 in Loeb) states that

Seleucus, after the partition of the kingdom of Antigonus, took his army to Phoenicia, which, in accordance with the terms of the agreement with Lysimachus and Cassander,[1] was to be his territory. Ptolemy, however, had already occupied the cities of that region when Antigonus left Antigoneia, and 'was denouncing Seleucus because, although he and Ptolemy were friends, Seleucus had accepted the assignment to his own share of a district that was already subject to Ptolemy; in addition, he accused the kings of giving him no part of the conquered territory, even though he had been a partner in the war against Antigonus. To these charges Seleucus replied that it was only just that those who were victorious on the battlefield should dispose of the spoils; but in the matter of Coele Syria, for friendship's sake he would not at present interfere, but would consider later how best to deal with friends who chose to encroach.' Coele Syria had been a core area of Antigonus' territory. Ptolemy had actually already invaded the region after the battle at Gaza and, before Ipsus, he had been besieging Sidon but had agreed to a four-month truce when false rumours led him to believe that Antigonus had defeated Lysimachus.

Thus, Seleucus, who had contributed decisively to the victory, ended up with the rather meagre gain of northern Syria and, according to Appian (*Syr.* 55), also 'inland Phrygia'.[2] His most important gain may actually have been a substantial part of Antigonus' army. A large number of these soldiers were probably Greeks and Macedonians already settled in Phoenicia and Palestine by Antigonus.

In this new political world, new alliances were formed. Justin (Pompeius Trogus XV.4) states that 'the allied generals, after thus terminating the war with the enemy, turned their arms again upon each other, and, as they could not agree about the spoil, were divided into two parties. Seleucus joined Demetrius, and Ptolemy joined Lysimachus.' Ptolemy and Lysimachus safeguarded their positions by a marriage alliance. Both men had married daughters of Antipater after Triparadeisus. During his campaign against Antigonus, Lysimachus had married Amastris of Heraclea in 302, and now he married Arsinoe, a daughter of Ptolemy. According to Plutarch (*Vit.Demtr.* 30–31), Lysimachus' son Agathocles married another

---

1   The agreement is mentioned by Polybius (V.67) in connection with negotiations between Antiochus III and ambassadors from Ptolemy V after Antiochus' conquest of Coele Syria and Phoenicia. Here, Antiochus refers to the agreement between Cassander, Lysimachus and Seleucus that this territory was to be allocated to Seleucus and thus stresses his own right to it.
2   See Grainger 1990, 159 for doubt about this.

of Ptolemy's daughters at the same time; however, other sources suggest that this marriage either took place earlier or not until later in the 290s.[3]

The quarrel over Coele Syria and the marriage alliance between Ptolemy and Lysimachus clearly left Seleucus feeling threatened, and this led him to approach Demetrius and enter into a marriage alliance with him. Thus Seleucus took Demetrius' daughter Stratonice as his bride. As Plutarch states, this was a piece of good luck for Demetrius, but it was also fortuitous for Seleucus. Unlike Ptolemy and Lysimachus, he had never been a member of the exclusive circle of the Macedonian elite, where marriage alliances were important features of general networking and political allegiances. As part of the wedding celebrations, Demetrius sailed to Syria with his whole fleet in 300 or 299.[4] His wife, Phila, probably with Stratonice, joined him from Cyprus, where she seems to have resided. Seleucus met him at Rhosus on the coast of northern Syria. Plutarch describes their interview as being carried out in a sincere and princely manner, without any indications of design or suspicion.

'Seleucus invited Demetrius first to his pavilion; and then Demetrius entertained him in his galley of 13 banks of oars. They conversed at their ease, and passed the time together without guards or arms, till Seleucus took Stratonice, and carried her with great pomp to Antioch. He had, indeed, already a son named Antiochus, by Apame, a Persian lady; but he thought that his dominions were sufficient for more heirs, and that he stood in need of this new alliance, because he saw Lysimachus marrying one of Ptolemaeus' daughters himself; and taking the other for his son Agathocles. A connection with Seleucus was a happy and an unexpected turn of fortune for Demetrius' (*Vit.Demtr.* 30–31).

On his way to the wedding, Demetrius had made several landings, probably with the intention of plundering, and in Cilicia he had marched up to Cyinda where he found 1,200 talents left in Antigonus' treasury. Thus Cilicia became one of Demetrius' possessions – no doubt with the consent of Seleucus.

That the alliance between Seleucus and Demetrius was a reality is indicated by a decree from Ephesus honouring Nikagoras of Rhodes, who had been sent on a goodwill mission to Ephesus and other Greek cities

---

3   See Dmitriev 2007.
4   Buraselis 1982, 59.

by Demetrius and Seleucus (*OGIS* 10).[5] The good terms between Demetrius and Seleucus were followed up, after relations had been restored between Seleucus and Ptolemy, with a marriage alliance between Demetrius and Ptolemy; Demetrius married Ptolemy's daughter Ptolemais (Plut. *Vit.Demtr.* XXXII.69).[6] Both Seleucus and Ptolemy, with his interests in Cyprus and the Aegean, must have considered it wise to maintain good terms with Demetrius. But Seleucus clearly also expected something in return for the alliance with Demetrius and soon demanded that he handed over to him Sidon and Tyre, which were still in his possession (and were later included in Ptolemy' kingdom), and also Cilicia.

The following passage of Plutarch's *Vit.Demtr.* is full of moral indignation that Seleucus should make such demands:

'Hitherto Seleucus had behaved with honour and propriety; but afterwards he demanded that Demetrius should surrender Cilicia to him for a sum of money, and on his refusal to do that, angrily insisted on having Tyre and Sidon. This behaviour appeared unjustifiable and cruel. When he already commanded Asia from India to the Syrian Sea, how sordid it was to quarrel for two cities with a prince who was his father-in-law, and who labored under so painful a reversal of fortune.'

But from Seleucus' point of view this made very good sense, both cities being among the most important in the eastern Mediterranean and situated in Phoenicia, to which he had laid claim though having accepted that, for the time being, it was part of Ptolemy's territory. Nonetheless, Demetrius refused Seleucus' claims by responding, according to Plutarch: '"Though I had lost a thousand battles as great as that at Ipsus, nothing should bring me to buy the alliance of Seleucus"; and upon this principle he garrisoned these cities in the strongest manner.'

Cassander died in 297, as king of Macedonia. The complex and ever-changing political scenario in Greece and Macedonia after Cassander's death had three principal characters: Demetrius, Pyrrhus of Epirus and Lysimachus (while Ptolemy too also played an important role).[7] Demetrius built up a large army and navy in order to reconquer his father's territories in Asia. He had already gathered 98,000 infantry and 12,000 cavalry, and had an enormous ship-building programme being

---

5 Walbank 1988, 206.
6 The marriage was actually fulfilled ten years later.
7 On these years in Macedonia, see Buraselis 1982; Walbank 1988.

fulfilled at Piraeus, Corinth, Chalcis and Pella. News of these activities reached the other kings and – probably sometime in 288[8] – they made an alliance against Demetrius; they also encouraged Pyrrhus to break his alliance with Demetrius, join them and attack Macedonia. In the spring of 287, Ptolemy sent a fleet to Greece in order to stir up a revolt, and Lysimachus invaded Macedonia and captured Amphipolis, while Pyrrhus invaded from the west. Demetrius was in Greece at the time, and an attempt to return to Macedonia and advance against Lysimachus ended with his army close to mutiny. Demetrius escaped to Cassandreia, where his wife Phila, in despair, committed suicide. Demetrius returned to Greece, and Lysimachus and Pyrrhus divided Macedonia between them. After some conflict, particularly over Athens, Ptolemy (who had gained Cyprus in 294 and now also the Cyclades, and had liberated Athens to some extent) now decided to withdraw from the alliance against Demetrius.

In probably the same year,[9] Demetrius received a message that Ptolemy had released Demetrius' wife and children, who had been held on Salamis, and sent them off with gifts and other honours (Plut. *Vit.Demtr.* XXXVIII) and in 294 he learnt that Seleucus had given Stratonice, with whom he had a daughter, Phila (who was later married to Antigonus Gonatas), in marriage to his son, Antiochus. In ancient literature this unusual act became a love story: it depicted the love of a father for a son who had fallen hopelessly in love with his young stepmother, Stratonice (Plut. *Vit. Demtr.* XXXVIII; App. *Syr.* 59–61). Antiochus had fallen seriously ill and his doctor told Seleucus that the illness was due to his unfulfilled love for Stratonice. Resolutely, Seleucus decided that Antiochus and Stratonice should be married and, as Plutarch reports, 'Upon this, Seleucus summoned the people to meet in full assembly, and told them it was his will and pleasure that Antiochus should intermarry with Stratonice, and that they should be declared king and queen of the Upper Provinces.' Seleucus was the only one of the Diadochs who had not married a Macedonian woman after the death of Alexander; he had continued his marriage with Apame, and her position was clearly that of a queen, as attested by an inscription from Miletus (Didyma inscriptions no. 8; for translation see Austin 2006, no. 51; see chapter 7). Thus, Seleucus' marriage to Stratonice must have been undertaken for purely political reasons, and so perhaps the story told by Plutarch and Appian may have a core of truth. That Seleucus loved his son and

---

8   Walbank 1988, 227.
9   Wallbank 1988, 214 n. 2, 232 n. 1.

wanted him as his successor is obvious. Antiochus had participated in the battle at Ipsus (see chapter 4), and the inscription from Miletus (see chapter 7) again attests to this. The award of the Upper Provinces was definitely not a means to exile Antiochus, as suggested, for instance, by Grainger (2014, 102–3); rather, it was an acknowledgement of Seleucus' trust in Antiochus and his ability to master this more difficult part of Seleucus' kingdom. And Antiochus turned out to be a very able viceroy of the eastern satrapies. He had spent most of his life in the east, and from his mother he had undoubtedly learnt the Persian language and customs. Our Greco-Roman sources fail to mention that Antiochus was half-Persian; apparently this was an issue of no interest, and thus discussion about him being only half Macedonian probably never arose.

After Demetrius had lost the throne of Macedonia, he decided to campaign against Lysimachus and so sailed to Asia late in 287 (Plut. *Vit. Demtr.*40). His army was down to 11,000 infantry and probably a similarly reduced cavalry and navy. He was met at Miletus[10] by Eurydice, who had brought her daughter Ptolemais in order that the marriage contract that had been agreed between Ptolemy and Demetrius, through Seleucus as an intermediary, could be fulfilled. Some of the cities of the region joined Demetrius, and he conquered others, such as the satrapal capital Sardis. Some of Lysimachus' officers deserted to him, bringing with them both troops and money. However, Lysimachus' son Agathocles fought a very able campaign against Demetrius and forced him into Phrygia, from where he intended to seize Armenia and then make an attempt on Media and the Upper Provinces, according to Plutarch (Plut. *Vit.Demtr.* XL.VI). Agathocles realised that he would not be able to beat Demetrius in battle and so instead he chose to cut off his supply convoys. As a consequence, levels of starvation grew worse in Demetrius' army every day, and later a plague broke out. Many men had also been lost in the fords of the Lycus river. Demetrius, aware that he had lost no less than 8,000 men, decided to turn back. He marched down to Tarsus, knowing full well that this was Seleucus' territory. Agathocles, however, blocked the Taurus pass and, at this turn of events, Demetrius felt forced to write a letter to Seleucus asking him 'to take compassion on a prince who was allied to him, and whose sufferings were such as even an enemy might be affected with' (Plutarch *Vit.Demetr.* 47).

---

10   Buraselis 1982, 100f. is sceptical about Miletus, and concludes that the marriage took place not in the city but in its vicinity.

According to Plutarch, Seleucus reacted positively and gave orders that supplies should be sent to Demetrius. At this point, Patrocles, the man perhaps closest to Seleucus (see chapter 6), warned him of the possible consequences of having Demetrius remain in his kingdom. Whether due to Patrocles' arguments or his own good sense, Seleucus ultimately decided to take a large army into Cilicia. Demetrius, surprised at this response, withdrew to the strongest position he could find on Mount Taurus and sent a messenger to Seleucus to beg to be allowed to conquer 'some of the free nations of barbarians, and by settling amongst them as their king, put an end to his wanderings. If this could not be granted, he hoped Seleucus would at least permit him to winter in that country, and not, by driving him out naked and in want of everything, expose him in that condition to his enemies' (*Vit.Demtr.* 47). This begging produced nothing but suspicion in Seleucus, and, according to Plutarch, he answered that Demetrius might stay two months of the winter in Cataonia, if he sent him his principal friends as hostages. Seleucus also secured the passes into Syria, and thus surrounded Demetrius 'like a wild beast in toils', as Plutarch writes. Demetrius now ravaged the country and apparently had the advantage whenever Seleucus attacked him. He broke through the pass into Syria and prepared for a decisive battle with Seleucus. According to Plutarch, Seleucus was seriously worried but declined an offer of support from Lysimachus. This detail is perhaps an invention of Plutarch's, designed to build suspense as his narrative draws to a climax.

Nonetheless, there was no climax to this episode; Demetrius was taken ill and his men began to desert. More than a month later he had recovered, and, feigning a move to Cilicia, he broke camp at night, crossed the Amanus mountains and ravaged the country as far into Syria as Cyrrhestica. Seleucus followed him and camped close to Demetrius. The latter's attempt to escape during the night failed, though not, according to Plutarch, without creating consternation in Seleucus' camp; the king is reported to have shouted to his men that a terrible wild beast was upon them. At dawn, Seleucus was ready for battle, but, instead of engaging the enemy, he changed his mind and came up with what we can now recognise as one of his typical schemes. He quit his horse and lay aside his helmet, and presented himself to Demetrius' mercenaries with only his shield in his hand. He exhorted them to come over to him and convinced them that it was to spare them, not Demetrius, that he had taken so long to engage in war. They all saluted him as king and joined his forces. Thus, totally humiliated, Demetrius fled to the passes of the Amanus and hid in a dense wood with a few friends, hoping to be able to escape to Caunus in

Lycia and find his fleet. In the end, his friends persuaded him to surrender to Seleucus. Plutarch recalls in detail, though perhaps not with great historical precision, how Seleucus treated Demetrius as a king, the father-in-law of, no longer himself, but his son Antiochus. Nonetheless, he had him firmly taken away to Apamea, where he was kept under strong guard, although with a retinue, money and a table suitable to his rank. According to Plutarch (*Vit.Demtr.* 51) he also had places to exercise and walk worthy of a king, his parks were well stocked with game and those friends who had accompanied him in his flight were permitted to attend him. Seleucus also let him know that as soon as Antiochus and Stratonice arrived, he might obtain his liberty.

Demetrius' son Antigonus (Gonatas), whom he had left in charge of his affairs in Greece, wrote to Seleucus and offered to hand over all his father's possessions and give himself as a hostage if he would set Demetrius free. According to Plutarch, many cities and princes added their names to this request, but not Lysimachus. According to Diodorus Siculus (XXI.20), Lysimachus sent ambassadors to Seleucus with the request that he should on no account release Demetrius from his power; he even offered to give Seleucus two thousand talents to do away with him, an offer that Seleucus strongly declined. To his son Antiochus, who was in Media, Seleucus wrote, advising him[11] how to deal with Demetrius. For he had previously decided to release him and restore him with great pomp to his throne, but wanted to give his son joint credit for this kindness.

Whether Antiochus and Stratonice ever had a say in this matter we do not know, but Demetrius remained in captivity for three years. He gradually sank into a deep depression, drinking excessively, and ultimately died. Plutarch, as always, offers his readers a dose of moral indignation at the fate of Demetrius (Plut. *Vit.Demtr.* 52):

'This was either because he sought escape from the thoughts on his recent condition which tormented him when he was sober and tried to smooth his reflections in drunkenness or because he had convinced himself that this was the real life which he had long desired and striven to attain but had foolishly missed it through folly and empty ambition, thereby bringing many troubles upon himself and many upon others; he had sought arms and fleets and armies to find the highest good, but now, to his surprise, had discovered it in idleness and leisure and repose. For what other end than this can worthless kings seek to attain by war and perils? Wicked

---

11   Or perhaps 'asking his advice': see Walton 1957, 39 n. 4 (Loeb), with reference to Dindorf.

and foolish indeed are they not only because they seek after luxury and pleasure instead of virtue and honour, but also because they do not even know real pleasure and true luxury.'

Demetrius' ashes were brought to Greece in an urn of solid gold and handed over to Antigonus Gonatas on one of the Aegean islands; they were later buried at Demetrias.

The last war that Seleucus was to fight was against Lysimachus. At the time of Demetrius' death in 283, Lysimachus' family relations had developed into a tragedy. He was at this time married to Arsinoe, a daughter of Ptolemy, who seems to have set the king up against his oldest son, Agathocles. Memnon is our best literary source for the tragic events that culminated in Seleucus and Lysimachus meeting each other as opponents on the battlefield. According to him, Arsinoe had made the old king suspicious of his oldest son, whom he decided to kill. First, he used poison, but Agathocles did not drink it, or rather spat it out; he was then thrown into prison where he was killed (Memnon 284). Pausanias (I.10.4) states that Agathocles' widow Lysandra, who was a sister of Arsinoe, together with her children and brothers now fled to Seleucus in Babylon and entreated him to make war on Lysimachus.

At this time, a half-brother of Arsinoe, Ptolemy Ceraunus, had fled to Lysimachus' court after his younger stepbrother of the same name had become his father's co-ruler in the last years of his reign. After the murder of Agathocles, he sided with his other sister, Lysandra, and fled with her to Seleucus. The murder of Agathocles and the split in Lysimachus' family resulted in unrest in Lysimachus' realm, with cities revolting against him (Memnon 12.6). For example, Philetaerus from Pergamum let Seleucus know that, if it came to war, he would side with Seleucus (Paus. I.10.4; Strabo XIII.4.1). Pergamum held one of Lysimachus' treasuries, and, according to Strabo, 9,000 talents were kept here. Seleucus must have felt that the time was ripe for a showdown with Lysimachus. None of our literary sources suggests that the two men were ever close to each other, despite both having campaigned with Alexander and later sided first with Antigonus against Eumenes and then with Ptolemy and Cassander against Antigonus. In fact, Plutarch (Vit.Demtr. LI) states that Seleucus had always felt an aversion to Lysimachus.

Thus, in the winter of 282/281, Seleucus invaded Lysimachus' Asian possessions. BCPH 9 lines 3–4, though very fragmentary, probably refer to Seleucus mustering his army in June to July 282 and setting out for Sardis, Lysimachus' capital in Asia Minor (see also Paus. I.10.4). This suggests that, by this time, Seleucus was staying in his eastern capital, though the years immediately after Ipsus probably saw him more or less settled in the western part of his realm, while Antiochus resided in the east. Babylon, however, is probably referred to here in only a general sense as the eastern capital, which by now was actually Seleucia-on-the-Tigris. According to Polyaenus (IV.9.4), during the course of his siege of Sardis Seleucus promised 100 talents to the soldier who opened the gate; Theodotus, Lysimachus' treasurer in the city, became worried that his own soldiers would kill him in order to obtain this reward, and so, in the end, he decided to open the gates himself.

We have little information about the final confrontation between these two giants of their day at Corupedium. The battle must have taken place in February or at the latest March 281.[12] According to Memnon, Lysimachus was killed in battle after being struck by the spear of a man from Heraclea, Malakon, who fought for Seleucus (Memnon 5). Appian (Syr.62) briefly states that Lysimachus was slain during the battle. Pausanias (I.X.4) reports that, Lysimachus' son Alexander after long negotiations with Lysandra, won his father's body and afterwards carried it to the Chersonesus and buried it, where his grave is still to be seen between the villages of Cardia and Pactye.

An inscription[13] from Aigai in Aiolis provides an interesting example of the honours that the city bestowed on Seleucus and Antiochus, probably shortly after their victory over Lysimachus in 281 (see chapter 7 for the inscription).

According to Memnon (8), Seleucus, encouraged by his success against Lysimachus, set out to cross over to Macedonia. 'He longed to return to his fatherland, from which he had set out with Alexander, and he intended to spend the rest of his life there, after handing over the government of Asia to his son Antiochus.'[14] Pausanias, in a more sober style, echoes this by reporting that Seleucus entrusted to Antiochus his entire empire in Asia, before heading towards Macedonia, followed by an army of both Greeks (probably to be understood as Greeks and Macedonians) and foreigners (I.XVI.2).

Both Memnon and the narrative of the *Babylonian Chronicle* (BCHP 9) place stress on the concepts of homeland and 'his land', and on Seleucus

---

12   Justin states that it took place seven months before the death of Seleucus, while BCHP 9 (two non-joining fragments from just below the middle of a tablet) records that Seleucus died in VI month (= 24 August to 26 September) 281.

13   The inscription was first published in 2009 by Malay and Ricl; also published in SEG 59.1406A; CGRN 137. Part of the inscription has been virtually effaced, since the block was reused as a threshold in an early Byzantine church at the site.

14   For a recent discussion of Seleucus' longing to go home, see Kosmin 2014, 82ff.

being a Macedonian; undoubtedly, both sources reflect a proclamation by Seleucus, which must have been made in connection with his entrusting all Asia to his son. Always pragmatic, Seleucus, at the brink of fulfilling his last ambition (which may not even have existed until the very moment of victory at Corupedium) and by now nearly 80 years old, knew that there was not much time left to him; thus, securing the position of his son must have been uppermost in his mind. Seleucus' decision to travel on to Europe may have been the standard follow-up of such a victory. He had now won Lysimachus' realm by the spear, and there were no rivals left to contest this.

Is it because we know what happened next that we feel something here is not quite 'business as usual'? For posterity, it is difficult to imagine that Seleucus was not gripped by the fact that he was the last of those highly able and ambitious high-ranking officers of Alexander who had spent more than 40 years fighting over Alexander's legacy. Was it a moment of triumph and deep satisfaction? Perhaps it was one of more mixed feelings? His appointment of Antiochus as king of Asia clearly indicates that this was a special moment, but it would have been anyway, taking into account Seleucus' age, something that he, ever the realist, would certainly have known and felt physically.

Thus, some months after his final victory, Seleucus set out for Europe. The army with which he travelled was probably a mix of his 'own' army and men from Lysimachus'. It is quite probable that he left behind most of his army with Antiochus. His close friend Patrocles seems not to have accompanied him to Europe, though he was probably with Seleucus at Sardis and on the battlefield. From the victory at Corupedium to his murder there is a time span of about seven months. According to the *Babylonian King List* of the Hellenistic period[15] Seleucus died in September 281.

Ptolemy Keraunus must have murdered Seleucus when the two were more or less alone. According to Appian (*Syr.* 62), this may have happened when they were on their way from the Hellespont to Lysimachaea, when Seleucus saw a 'great altar, which he was told had been built either by the Argonauts on their way to Colchis, or by the Achaeans who besieged Troy, for which the people in the neighbourhood still called it Argos, either by a corruption of the name of the ship Argo, or from a native place of the sons of Atreus. While he was learning these things he was killed by Ptolemy, who stabbed him in the back.' According to Memnon (8), Ptolemy then

---

15   https://www.livius.org/sources/content/mesopotamian-chronicles-content/
      babylonian-king-list-of-the-hellenistic-period/ See also Boiy 2011.

jumped on a horse and rode to Lysimachaea, where he put on a diadem and, escorted by a splendid bodyguard, returned to the army, who were then forced to accept him as king, 'though they had previously served under Seleucus'.

According to Appian (*Syr.* 63), Philetaerus, the dynast in Pergamum who had already, prior to Corupedium, indicated that he would follow Seleucus, purchased the body of Seleucus for a large sum of money, burned it and sent the remains to Seleucus' son Antiochus. The latter deposited them at Seleucia-by-the-Sea, where he raised a temple over them, around which he established a temenos; the temenos is called Nicotoreion. A Doric temple excavated at Seleucia may have been the Nicotoreion and Seleucus' last resting place.[16]

---

16 Hannestad and Potts 1990.

CHAPTER 6

Economy and administration

Information on the complex issues of the economy and administration of the Seleucid kingdom[1] is sparse throughout its entire existence, and for Seleucus and his time nothing more than glimpses, at best, can be seen of them. Here I attempt, first and foremost, to present sources from the time of Seleucus, but, in some instances, these concern other periods, such as that of Antigonus or Antiochus I. The formative period of the Seleucid kingdom is often particularly connected with Antiochus I but, undoubtedly, a solid foundation was laid in the period between Ipsus and the death of Seleucus. The years of co-regency between Seleucus and his son must have been decisive for the cohesion of the early Seleucid kingdom.

A matter of particular importance for all the kings and satraps would have been the economy of their territory. Since ancient times, Babylonia had been known to the Greeks as a rich and fertile region.[2] After Seleucus' return to his province in 311 (and later as king), it was essential for him to optimise his income in order to maintain sufficient resources for the military and the growing court, together with the large sums needed to fund his ambitious colonisation scheme (see chapter 8). His ability as both a general and a politician had led to the conquest of the other eastern satrapies in quick succession, followed by his campaign to India. By this time, his resources must have been enormous, despite the many years of war experienced by these territories.[3]

---

1 Recent discussions of these elements can be found in Capdetrey 2007; Aphergis 2004; van der Spek et al. 2015; see also Sherwin-White and Kuhrt 1993, 48f; for Achaemenid administration, Briant 2002, chapters 9–11.

2 See Herodotus III.82 for the tribute paid by Mesopotamia and Babylonia, which clearly indicates a fertile well-populated region. No less than 1,000 talents were paid as tribute each year.

3 According to Appian (*Syr.* 62), Seleucus had no less than 72 satrapies. But, if this is correct, a satrapy must have been a smaller unit than during the time of Alexander and the early years of the Diadochs. For a recent discussion of satrapies as administrative units, see Capdetrey 2007, 227ff with bibliography; a table of satrapies and satraps known by name during the period from Seleucus to Antiochus III is presented at Capdetrey 2007, 232–3.

Coinage

During the period of Alexander and the Diadochs, huge quantities of coins were minted to pay the armies. Babylonia was one of the few Achaemenid provinces that already had a silver-based economy, and, during Alexander's last years, large quantities of coins were minted there; in fact Baylonia was the location of the first mint east of the Euphrates. Large quantities were also minted for civil use, the upkeep of the court, gifts and benefactions from the king, etc. This structure of a coined-money-based economy was continued by Seleucus, who, in his first period as satrap, opened a second mint in Babylon[4] that produced tetradrachms and staters in the name of Philip III (as did the first mint, but with different dies and controls); this workshop seems to have been closed after Seleucus' flight. Following his return to Babylonia in 311, and particularly after he became king and initiated his great colonisation scheme, the need to optimise the royal income, and at the same time keep peace in the various regions of his realm, became even greater. Thus the second mint at Babylon was reopened. It produced two distinct types: an Alexander type, but with Seleucus' anchor symbol (see chapter 7), and a coinage of native type. The old mint from the time of Alexander continued to produce the Alexander type. The early Seleucids continued to monetise the economy of the empire to the greatest feasible extent, and as rapidly as possible, with coined money.[5] Mørkholm (1991, 24) has stressed that in the kingdoms the prime motivating factor regulating the volume of coinage was the rise and fall of public expenses. The growth of coined monetisation may be reflected on a microscale in Babylonia. Thus tablets from the Esagil record that in the early Hellenistic period astronomers were paid 180 litres of barley per month (see YBC 11549), whereas some very late texts (127–119 BC) inform us that they received an annual payment from the temple of 60–120 shekels of silver plus the revenue of some tracts of arable land.[6]

On gaining control of Susiana and Media, Seleucus continued the mint at Susa that Alexander had established in about 325.[7] The mint at Ecbatana seems to have been established immediately after Seleucus' conquest of Media (see chapter 4). Many other mints in the eastern satrapies (e.g. Ai Khanoum in Bactria) were established already under Seleucus

---

4   Houghton and Lorber 2002, XXII.
5   Aphergis 2004, 245.
6   See van der Spek, 1985. For commodity prices in Babylon 385–61BC, International Institute of Social History (http://www.iisg.nl/hpw/babylon.php); Beaulieu 2006.
7   Houghton Lorber 2002, 67.

Fig. 10 | *Tetradrachm.
Obverse head of Hera-
cles/Alexander with lion
helmet. Reverse Seated
Zeus and inscription
Dio; Alexandrou.
Minted in Alexandria
c. 325.*

or perhaps during the co-regency of Seleucus and Antiochus. A mint at Carrhae producing Alexander coins was probably founded under Antigonus and taken over by Seleucus, after whose death it seems to have been closed. Following the foundation of Seleucia-on-the-Tigris (see chapter 8), two mints were opened there within a few years, and the city produced enormous quantities of coins in silver, gold and bronze.

Gold was minted in staters, and very rarely in double staters, half staters and octodrachms. With a gold to silver ratio of 1:10, gold must have been reserved for special payments, such as those connected with the military or the administration or perhaps trade with India. [8] The production of gold coinage was much more frequent in the east than the west, where such coins are normally considered to have been minted for prestige or for military payments. That it may also have been used in other contexts, however, is evidenced by the Mnesimachus inscription from the Artemis temple at Sardis.[9] The extensive production of gold coins terminated at the end of the reign of Antiochus II.[10]

The silver tetradrachm (worth 1/5 of a gold stater) seems to account for 2/3 of the total value of coins produced, at least up to the reign of Antiochus III, and Aphergis considers it likely that this coin was the principal medium

---

8   See Aperghis 2004, 219.
9   Aperghis 2004, 320–3, Dossier 5, see below p. 86.
10 Aphergis 2004, 219.

of exchange in economic transactions between the administration and its subjects (2004, 220). The tetradrachm must also have been the main means of payment in regional, interregional and long-distance trade. Though bronze coins had been produced in the east since the reign of Seleucus I,[11] small denominations for daily use were also produced in silver: not only drachms but also hemidrachms, obols and hemiobols.

Hoards show that coins from the east, in particular from Babylon and Seleucia, found their way to the west in significant numbers during the lifetime of Seleucus. The few hoards found in the east, on the other hand, generally contain coins from the eastern provinces only.[12] An interesting hoard from al-ʿAyun in central Arabia,[13] however, shows a completely different pattern, with coins from a geographical spread covering Macedonia to Babylon. This seems to evidence a visit from Seleucid soldiers, carrying payments from several territories of Alexander's empire. A similar pattern is also seen in a coin hoard from Failaka.[14]

After Ipsus and the establishment of Seleucus' new foundations in northern Syria (see chapter 8), a number of mints were established in some of these cities; first and foremost amongst these was the one at Antioch, which became the main mint in the western part of the empire. The number of coins issued in the west during Seleucus' reign was small compared with the number emanating from the east; this clearly shows that coins were already abundant in the latter area, with only a limited need for new ones.[15] Large numbers of bronze issues attest to the long tradition of coined money in the west.

The Oikonomika

The *Oikonomika* of Pseudo Aristotle is a treatise on government finance (*oikonomia*) in three parts; the second was not written by the same person as parts I and III[16]. The treatise covers royal, satrapal, city-state and individual household finances. It was probably composed during the last quarter of the fourth century by a person familiar with the Persian economic system and the period of Alexander. It may actually have been composed during Seleucus' reign.

---

11 See B. Kritt in Houghton and Lorber 2002, 5ff.
12 Houghton and Lorber 2002, 107.
13 Potts 2010, 68.
14 Amandry and Callot 1988, 64–74; see also Hannestad 2019.
15 For a table, now probably somewhat obsolete, of the pattern of Seleucid coinage issues, see Aperghis 2004, 217 and for a similar table, see Houghton and Lorber 2002, Appendix 4, 133–156.
16 See Isager 1988,77; van Groningen and Wartelle 1968, XII–XIII.

In the *Oikonomika*, the royal economy is divided into four elements. The first is described as coinage (*nomisma*), and covers, amongst other things, 'what to mint of large or small denominations'.[17] This clearly indicates that the Greek system, of coined money, was common practice by the time the treatise was written. The other elements are imports, exports[18] and expenditures ('what is to be cut and when, and whether to meet expenses with coin or with goods in place of coin').[19] The royal economy evidently had unlimited power, and a characteristic example of this, in terms of raising resources, dates from the early period of the Diadochs when Antigonus was at war against Ptolemy, Seleucus and Lysimachus:[20] the former ordered a fleet to be built in Phoenicia. Antigonus called for a meeting with the kings of the Phoenicians and the hyparchs of Syria (Diod. Sic. XIX.58). The kings were instructed to assist him in building the ships and the hyparchs were ordered to gather together quickly four and a half million measures of wheat. He undertook personally to gather together woodcutters, carpenters and shipwrights from all over, and had the wood carried to the sea from Lebanon. There were 8,000 men employed in cutting and sawing the timber and 1,000 pairs of draught animals used to transport it. The ships were built in three different shipyards in Phoenicia and a fourth in Cilicia.

According to the *Oikonomika*, the most important instrument in the royal economy was that of revenue/tribute, of which there was a wide variety. The royal and satrapal economies were clearly closely linked, and the satrapal tasks are described as being concerned with six different classes of revenue: those arising from the land, from private production in the country, from market centres, from dues, from herds and flocks, and from other sources.[21]

Resources

As in most regions in Antiquity, the main resources of Seleucus' provinces emanated from agriculture. Land in Babylonia seems to have been classified into three or four categories (all in principle owned by individuals):

---

17 Translation Aperghis 2004, 119.
18 For a discussion of the terms *eisagogima* and *exagogima*, see Aperghis 2004, 119; see also Briant 2002, 452, where he argues that these terms are connected with the royal storehouses.
19 Translation Aphergis 2004, 121.
20 DS XIX.58 undoubtedly taken from Hieronymus.
21 Translation Aphergis 2004, 122. See Aperghis 2004, 122 for a discussion of the translations by Armstrong and by van Groningen and Wartelle. For a quick overview of the different types of economy, see https://en.wikipedia.org/wiki/Economics_(Aristotle).

royal land (land of the king), temple land (land of god X or god Y) and private land. There was also a category of land with no owner, but that could probably be claimed easily as royal land. [22]

We have no evidence that Seleucus or, later, Antiochus attempted to take over temple land; Seleucus must have been aware that such attacks on the temples and their rights would only have produced opposition and unrest among the local population. That disputes could arise though is evidenced by a tablet in the British Museum,[23] which contains a judgement by a royal official in Babylon concerning a dispute between the royal treasury and the Ebabbar temple (probably in Sippar) concerning the land of Ebabbar. The text is dated to the desperate year of 308/307 and, though incomplete, enough is preserved to comprehend that the royal treasury gave up its claim on the temple's land and the temple gave up its claim to half the harvest (barley) which was to be handed over to the treasury. Thus the king got what he needed most, and the temple kept its land.

Crops, market prices, etc.

For Babylonia the *Astronomical Diaries*[24] offer extremely valuable information concerning market prices of a number of commodities. [25] The list encompasses several hundred centuries, including the Hellenistic period. The prices are mentioned on tablets written by Babylonian astronomers; one tablet (YBC 11549) from the early Hellenistic period mentions that at least 14 astronomers were fully employed by the Marduk temple/Esagil to make astronomical observations. Here I follow the interpretations of the prices given by Aperghis 2004 and van der Spek et al. 2015. The agricultural products mentioned are barley, dates, mustard, sesame, cress and wool.[26] The *Astronomical Diaries* clearly indicate that barley, which must have formed the staple diet of both the men (when wheat was not available) and horses of the armies of Alexander and his successors reached very high prices on the market [27] in the late fourth and the first half of the third cen-

---

22 Van der Spek 1995, 189ff.

23 Van der Spek 1995, 194–5, text 9.

24 Sachs and Hunger 1988.

25 See Temin 2002, 46–60; Aphergis 2004, 78ff, van der Spek 2008.

26 In modern times, wheat is also grown in Iraq, and probably already in antiquity in northern Mesopotamia and also in the drier irrigated zones further south as a winter crop together with barley (see Iraq Salinity Project technical report no. 8 Report B2.1: historical agricultural production data in Iraq https://www.icarda.org/media/news/reviving-iraq-through-conservation-agriculture. However, wheat is not mentioned in the Babylonian texts as a market crop.

27 I follow van der Spek et al. 2015, 2–3 in accepting the broad definition of 'market', as used in new institutional economics, as being suitable also for discussions of ancient markets.

tury.[28] Aperghis suggests various military or political reasons for high prices in different years. Recently, Huijs and Pirngruber (2015), studying the second century BC, have introduced climate change as yet another factor for the changing market prices of barley and other types of goods in Babylonia; and, of course, there were, as always, good years and bad years of harvest. Furthermore, the hosting over long periods of a large army with its specific needs, despite there being no military action, must have put pressure on the system.

A good example is the year 322, when the market price of barley rose steeply for what seems like the whole year,[29] and the price of dates also rose substantially. This is the year following Alexander's death, when Perdiccas and Seleucus stayed on in Babylon with a large portion of the royal army. A passage in Diodorus Siculus, clearly adopted directly from Hieronymus, reports that Eumenes had his army live on sesame, dates and rice following their arriving in Susiana, where no grain was available (see chapter 4), 'since the land produced such fruits as these in plenty' (XIX.13). The barley harvest is in April, whereas dates and rice are summer crops, and this fits well with Eumenes being unable to obtain enough grain on the march to Susa. The year of the last phase of the Babylonian War again saw drastic rises in prices of both barley and dates. According to the *Babylonian Chronicle* (BCHP 3), the years 309 and 308 brought 'weeping and mourning in the land'; famine had probably broken out. The price of barley rose to a shekel for 6 litres; normally, more than 100 litres could be purchased for one shekel. After this, prices seem to have remained fairly stable throughout the remainder of Seleucus' reign.

Forestry and metal resources may have been exclusively under royal control. Seleucus soon controlled the forests of the Zagros mountains and, after Ipsus, those of the Taurus mountains too. In terms of precious metals, although the Seleucid kingdom was not rich in gold, there must have been enough available for the extensive minting of gold coins under the early Seleucids (see, e.g., Strabo XI.8.6). Silver, iron and copper may also to a large extent have come from Bactria.[30]

---

28 See Aperghis 2004, fig. 5.2 (note that the graph goes up when the prices go down); see also Foldvari and van Leeuwen 2015, 26 fig. 2.1.
29 See Appendix in van der Spek et al. 2015.
30 See https://en.wikipedia.org/wiki/Mining_in_Afghanistan#Gold

Revenue

In most areas, the most important sources of revenue were undoubtedly those raised from the land and their products. The annual tribute to be paid on land is reflected in the often-discussed Mnesimachos inscription,[31] which was found in the Artemis temple at Sardis and records that Antigonus gave several pieces of land to Mnesimachos. Apparently, Mnesimachus had obtained a loan from the Artemis temple at Sardis; he was unable to repay the debt and his property was thus to be taken over by the temple. The tax (*phoros*) payable for various areas that included one or more village is detailed, and varies from 57 gold staters to 3 gold staters. Each tax was paid to a specific chiliarchy, which in this period must have been an administrative unit. The total value of the estate was 2,650 gold staters, plus eventually the value of the annual harvest of grain and fruit. Further conditions were set up. Thus, if the king took from Artemis the estate due to Mnesimachos, he and his descendants must repay the original loan of 1,325 staters. The inscription was set up on the interior of the northwestern ante wall of the temple. The date must be later than the erection of this part of the temple, but both the date of the temple and the inscription have been much debated; the temple building itself may have been initiated after Ipsus by Lysimachus or by Seleucus/Antiochus after Corupedium.

Like the Achaemenid kings, the Seleucid rulers also granted land to their friends (see below) and other high-ranking individuals. Most land was probably given in usufructus, i.e. benefit could be derived from use of the land, but the land itself still belonged to the king. But under the Seleucids the recipient of royal land could attach it to a city, decided on either by the king or by the recipient (this phenomenon is seen at least in Asia Minor), and thus remove it from direct royal control. Although we have no evidence directly related to Seleucus concerning this issue, there is a relevant and well preserved inscription from the time of Antiochus I erected at Ilium (RC10-13; Aphergis 2004,101–2, Document 2, 312–5). The inscription contains a dossier of letters: (1) from Meleager, Antiochus' deputy in Asia Minor to the boule of Ilium; (2) from King Antiochus to Meleager; (3) a second letter from the king to Meleager; and (4) a third letter from the king to Meleager. The correspondence concerns a certain Aristodicus of Assos, a friend of Antiochus who had asked the king for more land in the Hellespontine in addition to what he had already received. The king responded positively and ordered Meleager to find 2,000 plethra of cultivable land to

---

31 See Billows 1995, III-45; Aphergis 2004, 320ff.

be attached to either Ilium or Scepsis. Apparently, Aristodicus then asked for more land, more specifically the village of Petra and 1,500 plethra of its cultivable land and another 2,000 plethra of cultivable land bordering it, 'because he has provided services to us as our friend with goodwill and eagerness'. The inscription offers an interesting glimpse of a bureaucracy that depended on local information. Here we have the king asking if the specific piece of land was available, only to discover that it had already been given away – to an Athenaeus, commander of the naval base. Aristodicus received a different piece of land, 'which he may join to any of the cities in our alliance he wishes'. Aristodicus decided to attach his land to Ilium, and therefore the whole correspondence was sent to the boule and assembly of Ilium by Meleager, who admonished them to do what Aristodicus asked of them and to vote him the full range of privileges. Land, at least in western Asia Minor, seems to have been classified in two categories: crown land and city land. In other regions, there was also temple land, an old phenomenon, not least in the Near East (see above).

Land given or sold by the king to individuals, could be exempted from part of the tribute or the tribute right could be transferred to the person receiving the land, as in the case of the Laodice inscription found in Didyma, in which the value is stated in silver talents. Laodice (the ex-wife of Antiochus II) had bought a specific piece of land, including a village and a mansion, from her ex-husband.[32] She was allowed to attach the land to whichever city she wished. In this case, stelae detailing this information were to be set up not only in the temple of Athena at Ilium, but also in the temple of the Gods on Samothrace, the Artemis temples at Sardis and Ephesus, and the temple of Apollo at Didyma.

The salt tax figures prominently in the archaeological evidence of taxation from the Seleucid kingdom; it is attested through finds of large numbers of scal impressions, e.g. in Seleucia on the Tigris and Uruk. One impression found in Seleucia by the Michigan expedition dates from 286/285[33] (i.e. to the period of the co-regency of Seleucus and Antiochus) and records *halikes*, year and name of city. *Halikae* are salt pans, and here the reference must be to a tax related to salt. Salt pans were probably under royal control and every household had to buy a certain number at a fixed price.[34] Later, most of these bullae were marked with *epitelon* (= taxed) or *atelon* (= tax-free).

---

32 RC 18-20; Aperghis 2004, 315–8.
33 McDowell 1935, 198.
34 See Aperghis 2004, 155.

Both in Seleucia and Uruk, many of the bullae concern sales connected with the river port.[35] Undoubtedly, tax on goods transported by river was, at least in Mesopotamia, a lucrative business for the king. Both cities also show evidence for a tax on slaves, in particular imported slaves. That the king could exempt a city from taxes and also reward a city in special cases is attested during the period of Antiochus III. An example is a letter from the king to the inhabitants of Jerusalem, rewarding them for their support during the Fifth Syrian War; the rewards ranged from sacrificial animals, wine, oil and frankincense, wheat and salt for religious purposes, to support for the rebuilding of the temple and a number of tax exemptions and reductions (including head taxes, crown taxes and salt taxes). That the system dates back to the times of Seleucus and Antiochus I is attested by dedications to Didyma and Miletus though here in a different form (see chapter 7).

The last part of book 2 of the *Oikonomika* is a long list detailing how to collect taxes, and the latest examples belong to the time of Alexander. One of them tells of Antimenes from Rhodes, whom Alexander had appointed superintendent (= uncertain Greek term: see Armstrong 1962, 390) of highways in the province of Babylon, reviving an old law of the country allowing a tax on goods brought into the city: 'An ancient law of the country imposed a tax of one-tenth on all imports; but this had fallen into total abeyance. Antimenes kept a watch for all governors and soldiers whose arrival was expected, and upon the many ambassadors and craftsmen who were invited to the city, but brought with them others who also dwelt there unofficially; and also upon the multitude of presents that were brought (to these persons), on which he collected the legal tax of a tenth.'[36] The same official is also mentioned as having invented a payment of eight drachms per year per slave that soldiers had in the camp, as a kind of insurance. If a slave ran away, Antimenes instructed the satrap of the province in which the camp lay either to recover the man or to pay his master his value.

Furthermore, Antimenes ordered the satraps to keep the storehouses along the royal roads filled according to the custom of the country. Whenever an army or any other body of unaccompanied men passed along one of these roads he would send one of his own men to sell the contents of the storehouses,[37] thus marketing the wheat from the royal granaries. The practice was continued by Antigonus (and undoubtedly Seleucus), as attested

---

35 Invernizzi 2004; Lindström 2003.
36 Translation Armstrong 1962.
37 Pseudo Aristotle II.38; see Briant 2002, 453.

by an inscription from western Asia Minor: [38] 'In the past we did not desire
to give any city the right of importing grain or of creating a reserve store of
grain, because we did not wish the cities to spend money on these things
which were often not necessary. And neither did we desire this now, as
the taxed land is close by, so that, if there were need for grain, we believe
that as much as necessary could easily be requested to be brought from it.'[39]
Thus, the king could benefit from a market nearby (a Greek city) by selling
surplus wheat derived from tribute.[40] Another early Hellenistic inscription,
dating from 317 from the city of Nasos, is a decree in honour of a Thersip-
pus and records that, in addition to other benefactions towards Nasos, he
had obtained from the satrap the right to import wheat (OGIS 4; Briant
2002, 453). Briant argues convincingly that this practice was inherited from
the Achaemenid period and refers to an Athenian decree honouring the
satrap Orontes for selling wheat to the city (*IG* II.2 207a; see *AIO IG* II.3 1
295, tentatively dated to 348/349 BC). As noted by van der Spek (2007, 431),
royal decrees were the only unifying element in the Seleucid legal system;
otherwise, local systems continued in existence, although they could be
overruled by royal legislation.

Friends

Friends of kings played an important role in all the new Hellenistic kingdoms.[41] The system of friendship existed in Macedonia and was continued
by Alexander on his eastern campaign. To a large extent, the friends made
up the higher military and administrative class responsible to the king for
running his kingdom.[42] The Seleucid kingdom as created by Seleucus was
a military monarchy. It was not a constitutional entity;[43] rather it had a core
consisting of the king, his friends and the military (see, e.g., OGIS 11 from
Priene to Lysimachus and his army; *Inschriften von Magnesia* 86 to king
Attalus, queen Stratonice, his brothers, friends and his army). The rela-
tionships between kings and their friends were built on gift exchange; the
friends were expected to be loyal and carry out tasks that the king wished to
be performed; in return they received rich gifts from the king, as attested by

---

38 *RC* 3; Aperghis 2004, 310, Document 1.
39 Translation Aperghis 2004, 311.
40 Briant 2002, 453.
41 For recent studies of the phenomenon, see Savalli-Lestrade 1998; Strootman 2014, in particular chapter 5.
42 See Thompson 1997, 97ff.
43 Austin 2003, 124.

the Mnesimachus inscription (Antigonus, see above) and the example of Aristodicus (Antiochus, see above).

One of the ways in which friendship could be achieved in the early Diadoch period is demonstrated by Diodorus Siculus, who reports how

'Antigonus summoned Hieronymus, the historian and a friend and fellow citizen of Eumenes of Cardia, who had taken refuge in the stronghold called Nora. After endeavouring to attach Hieronymus to himself by great gifts, he sent him as envoy to Eumenes, urging the latter to forget the battle that had been fought against him in Cappadocia, to become his friend and ally, to receive gifts many times the value of what he had formerly possessed and a greater satrapy, and in general to be the first of Antigonus' friends and his partner in the whole undertaking.[44] Antigonus also at once called a council of his friends and, after he had made them acquainted with his design for gaining imperial power, assigned satrapies to some of the more important friends and military commands to others; and by holding up great expectations to all of them, he filled them with enthusiasm for his undertakings. Indeed he had in mind to go through Asia, remove the existing satraps, and reorganize the positions of command in favour of his friends' (XVIII.50.4–5).

Clearly, satraps, like the later kings, could also employ friends, and the friends could be of various ranks and levels of importance. The highest-ranked friends were generals and satraps, who also formed the king's *synedrion*.[45]

The first we hear of Seleucus' friends is after he arrives at Ptolemy's court following his escape from Babylon, when he sends 'certain friends to Europe to convert Lysimachus and Cassander into enemies of Antigonus' (Diod. Sic. XIX.56). Later, we hear further of his friends when, on his way from Egypt to Babylon, Seleucus is reported as stating that he would have made the expedition into the interior with the company of just his friends and his own slaves (Diod. Sic.XIX.90.1; see chapter 4).

Our knowledge of Seleucus' friends is very limited, and only a few names are known to us from the written sources.[46] Patrocles, Seleucus' most trusted general, may actually have accompanied him back to Babylon in 312.[47] He followed Seleucus and Antiochus on the campaign against Lysimachus, but stayed with Antiochus when Seleucus set out on his fateful

---

44 At the same time, according to Diodorus Siculus (XIII.53.2–7), Eumenes had no less than 500 friends besieged with him in the Nora fortress.

45 Strootman 2014, chapter 5.

46 See Savalli-Lestrade 1998, 3–10; Capdetrey 2007, 232; Strootman 2014, 130.

47 Kosmin 2014, 67.

journey to Macedonia. During the co-regency, he was assigned command over Bactria and Sogdiana, according to Strabo (II.1.17). He also received the task of undertaking a *periplus* of the Caspian Sea, a project that had been one of Alexander's last wishes and that was now carried out by his successor (Arr. *Anab.* VII.16.1–3). The record of the *periplus* of Patrocles is not preserved, but it seems to have profoundly influenced later geographers. According to Patrocles, the Caspian Sea was a bay (*kolpos*) of the ocean, whereas Herodotus had already clearly characterised it as a lake (Herodotus *Histories* 1.203; Strabo II.5 probably reflects Patrocles' report).

Demodamas of Miletus functioned as ambassador from the king to Miletus (see chapter 7) and also as a general for both Seleucus and Antiochus. He made an expedition to northern Sogdiana, reaching the Iaxartes, where he raised an altar for the Didymean Apollo. Apollonides, son of Charops and possibly from Cyzicus (see Plut. *Life of Demetrius* L.3), who had been a friend of Antigonus and Demetrius but had joined Seleucus at some point, was in 286/285 sent by Seleucus to Demetrius after Demetrius' final defeat in order that the latter should feel more at ease. Daimachus from Plataea is mentioned by Strabo (II.1.9) as ambassador to India and author of several works on India, and was probably also a friend of Seleucus. Megathenes, who was a Greek from Asia Minor and seems first to have lived at the court of the satrap Sibyrtius, apparently became Seleucus' ambassador to Chandragupta Mayrya (Sandracottus) and wrote an *Indica*, which is unfortunately not preserved;[48] he too was probably a friend.

The issue of whether only Macedonians and Greeks were counted among the friends of the Hellenistic kings, as was the case under Alexander, has been much debated. According to Savalli-Lestrade,[49] the friends of the Hellenistic kings also seem mainly to have been Macedonians and Greeks. However, based on the preserved names, it is undoubtedly incorrect to assume that all of them were. Men from Babylonia sometimes received a Greek name,[50] and it is quite possible, in my opinion, that among the lower ranks of friends working in their local areas were both Persians and Babylonians who had perhaps changed their original names. Seleucus, as far as we know, was on good terms with high-ranking Babylonians, and probably also Persians; his son was half Persian and his wife, Apame, was a member of the Persian aristocracy. On the other hand, he was very proud of being

---

48 See Kosmin 2014, 37–58; Wiesehöfer et al. 2016.
49 Lestrade 1998, 215-236.
50 Sherwin-White and Kuhrt 1993, 150ff.

a Macedonian, and it is possible that these high-ranking Babylonians and Persians were given other titles.

A central issue with regard to economy and administration is to what extent the Seleucid kingdom was a continuation of practices from the Achaemenid period.[51] Undoubtedly, much of the Achaemenid administration was continued under both Alexander and the Seleucids. Our main sources for the Achaemenid economic system are Herodotus, Xenophon and Pseudo Aristotle, together with the two Persepolis archives: the Fortification Tablets (509–494 BC) and the Treasury Tablets (492–458 BC).[52] There were, however, significant changes. One was the change in administrative language from (Imperial) Aramaic to Greek, whilst another was to coined monetisation.

---

51   See Sherwin-White and Kuhrt 1993; Briant 2002; van der Spek 2006/2007, 432.
52   See Briant 2002, part 3.

CHAPTER 7

Royal propaganda and ideology

Alexander was Seleucus' role model to a greater extent, probably, than for any of the other Diadochs, but not in the sense that this pragmatic man saw himself as Alexander reborn. Unlike Ptolemy, he could not boast of having buried Alexander, but the literary sources state that he was proud to have fought with Alexander throughout the duration of his campaign, and he clearly used this fact as propaganda. Seleucus combined the talent of a great general with the ambition to re-establish Alexander's Asian kingdom. After all, Seleucus' realm covered the major part of Alexander's empire after 301. He also seems to have shared Alexander's instinct for attracting loyalty, and his understanding of foreign peoples and their customs seems obvious, probably assisted by the influence of his wife, Apame, a Persian aristocrat. He may not only have understood but also spoken Aramaic, as undoubtedly did his son. In short, no identical model of kingship operated elsewhere in the Hellenistic world.[1]

Thonemann (2015, 146) has identified royal ideology as 'a set of widespread popular beliefs about a king's status and role: his quasi-divine nature, his generosity as benefactor, his charismatic authority and personal courage in warfare'. In what follows, I examine a number of objects related to Seleucus in which a royal ideology is clearly visible.

Coins

Coins were the principal media used by the Diadochs to spread their ideology, since they had the furthest reach.[2] The general pattern of continuity from Alexander to Seleucus is reflected in the latter's early coins: large

---

1   Sherwin-White and Kuhrt 1993, 114.
2   See also Thonemann 2015, 145-146.

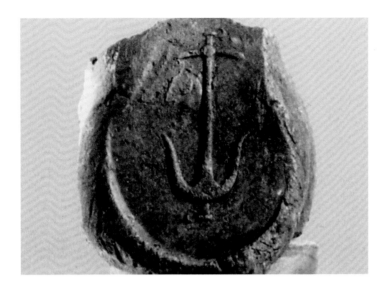

Fig. 11 | *Stamp impression from Seleucia-on-the-Tigris showing Seleucus' anchor.*

quantities of Alexander coins in the name of Philip III were minted during his first period as satrap in Babylon, not only in the mint that Alexander had established here but also in a second mint that Seleucus opened during at this time (see chapter 6). This fits well with his response to Eumenes (see chapter 3) that he was willing to assist the kings, but not Eumenes; here, Seleucus' loyalty to the Argeads and the elected king is clear.[3]

Seleucus' first personal mark on coins seems to have been the anchor, which appeared on Alexandrines with Philip's name ascribed to a workshop in Babylon during his second period as satrap.[4] The condition of some of these coins seems to suggest that the anchor has been removed from them. Houghton and Lorber suggest that this happened while Antigonus was in Babylon (2002, 43); if this was the case, it would mean that the anchor was employed on coins already during Seleucus' first period as satrap. The so-called native or satrapal mint in Babylon, which Alexander had permitted to function under Mazaeus and which issued a coinage with Baal and the lion, now employed an anchor above a lion on the reverse.[5] Appian explains the adoption of the anchor symbol: 'It was said also that in Macedonia a great fire burst forth on his ancestral hearth without anybody light-

---

3   See Houghton and Lorber 2002, xxxiii.
4   For a discussion, see Houghton and Lorber 2002, XXXIII, 3, 43–4.
5   See Houghton and Lorber 2002, pl. 8, 144.

ing it; also that his mother saw in a dream that whatever ring she found she should give him to carry, and that he should be king at the place where he should lose the ring. She did find an iron ring with an anchor engraved on it, and he lost it near the Euphrates' (*Syr.* 56). According to Arrian, it was also said that at a later period, when he was returning to recover Babylon, Seleucus stumbled against a stone and that when he had this stone dug up an anchor was found under it. 'When the soothsayers were alarmed at this prophecy, thinking that it portended delay, Ptolemy, the son of Lagus, who accompanied the expedition, said that an anchor was a sign of safety, not of delay. For this reason Seleucus, when he became king, used an engraved anchor for his signet-ring'.

The most important announcement made by each of the Diadochs who proclaimed himself king was a change of coin inscription: their names replaced those of Alexander and Philip III Arrhidaeus. Thus the first mint at Seleucia-on-the-Tigris, probably beginning in about 300 BC, produced Alexander types in its early years (gold staters, silver tetradrachms) with Seleucus' name. Just after 300,[6] Ptolemy began to mint coins with his own portrait instead of that of Heracles/Alexander. Demetrius immediately followed this example, although Antigonus, Lysimachus and possibly (see below) also Seleucus did not.

The first reference to elephants on the coins of the Diadochs was the portrayal of Alexander with an elephant headdress, instead of a lion skin, produced by Ptolemy on tetradrachms. This probably occurred at the time of the arrival of Alexander's body in Egypt or shortly after, when Ptolemy had outmanoeuvred Perdiccas, or the time of the meeting at Triparadeisus.[7] Seleucus adopted this motif in Babylon, Susa and Ecbatana, where gold darics with Alexander wearing an elephant headdress on the obverse and a standing Nike on the reverse were struck.[8] Furthermore, the first mint in Seleucia-on-the-Tigris produced bronze coins with a combination of the head of Athena on the obverse and an elephant on the reverse.[9]

In Susa, a series of tetradrachms and drachms, minted from around 305/304, or possibly some years later, and ending in about 295 (dating based on hoard evidence), display on the obverse a helmet-clad male head wearing a panther skin (fig. 12). The helmet is covered with the skin and adorned with the horns and ears of a bull. The reverse shows a Nike crowning a trophy. This coin probably celebrates Seleucus' victories in the east.

---

6   Mørkholm 1991, 66.
7   Lorber 2005, 62.
8   Houghton and Lorber 2002, Babylon no. 101, Susa no. 183, Ecbatana no. 219.
9   Houghton and Lorber 2002, nos 128-129.

Fig. 12 | *Tetradrachm minted at Susa. Obverse male head with panther skin helmet fitted with bull's ear and horns. Reverse Nike erecting a trophy.*

The head has often been identified as Dionysus,[10] though the iconography is far removed from the traditional portrayal of Dionysus. Stewart (1993, 314–5) suggests that it is actually a portrait of Alexander. This conclusion, however, does not explain the bull's horns. Houghton and Lorber (2002) suggest the image is a combination of Dionysus, Alexander and Seleucus. Hoover (2002), meanwhile, argues more convincingly that it is indeed a portrait of Seleucus, after his anabasis to India. Victory is suggested by the Nike with a trophy on the reverse. Thus Seleucus was apparently portrayed and, like other Diadochs, given divine honours during his lifetime (see also below). The type is found virtually only in Persis. Hoover (2011) also argues that the employment of bull imagery in connection with Seleucus I sent a deliberate message to the local populations of Babylonia and Iran, stating that the king connected himself with them, in contrast to Antigonus and Alexander. However, bulls and bull horns are also Greek cultural motifs, and we see coins depicting Demetrius with bull horns.[11]

The main ideological motif of Seleucus' royal mints in the east was the elephant quadriga or biga with Athena driving.[12] This emerged from a second workshop set up in Seleucia around 296/295, where it was used as a

---

10   E.g. Hadley 1974.

11   Mørkholm 1991, fig. 172.

12   Alexander on an elephant quadriga is seen on gold staters of Ptolemy, see, e.g., Mørkholm 1991, no. 96.

Fig. 13 | *Reverse of tetra-drachm showing Athena fighting with shield and spear on a war chariot drawn by two elephants. On the obverse the coins show a head of Zeus. Minted at Susa.*

reverse motif. On the obverse, the Heracles/Alexander head was replaced with a head of Zeus, as employed in Macedonia under Philip II and during the early years of Alexander. In a Near Eastern context, this image could perhaps be identified also with Baal or another principal god. The elephant quadriga motif was also used on coins from Susa and Bactria[13] and, as a symbolic motif, it sits well with Demetrius' nickname for Seleucus: 'Ele-phantarchos'.

A further motif that is also closely linked to Seleucus is the horned horse head. The intended message of this image has been much debated. The head has frequently been identified as representing Bucephalus, Alex-ander's famous horse, though why this should be the case has never been explained adequately. Recently, Miller and Walters (2004) have suggested that the horns reflect a Near Eastern tradition in which they signify roy-alty and divinity, as previously suggested by other scholars, and that the horse is not intended to represent Bucephalus. The first appearance of this motif seems to have been on a gold stater from Susa, where, according to Houghton and Lorber, it is a Seleucid symbol (2002, no. 160). On the obverse there is a head of Athena in a helmet and on the reverse a stand-ing Nike and the inscription *Alexandrou Basileos*. The motif is also seen

13 See, e.g., Ai Khanoum (Houghton and Lorber 2002, 276–7). Houghton and Lorber consider the motif to be characteristic for the eastern part of the empire (2002, 52).

on a series of silver tetradrachms of the Alexandrine type from Susa, with a seated Zeus on the reverse, that was struck soon after 311 according to Houghton and Lorber (2002, 7). Later, it is seen on coins from Babylon, Susa, again, and Ecbatana. As a separate motif, it was employed by a mint in Bactria, Aria or Margiana, with an anchor on the reverse,[14] and was used on late coins from Pergamum and other cities in western Asia Minor celebrating the victory at Corupedium.[15] The Pergamum issues have an elephant on the reverse. An explanation for the inclusion of the horned horse head may be that the horse should be identified with the one on which Seleucus escaped from Babylon as he fled from Antigonus. According to Malalas, Seleucus erected a monument outside Antioch, on the other side of the river, consisting of a gilded horse's head and a helmet together with an inscription that read: 'On this Seleucus escaped to safety from Antigonus; and returning from there he killed Antigonus'.[16]

The head of Seleucus with bull horns[17] can be found on gold staters, tetradrachms and drachms. These coins are attributed by Kritt (1996) and Houghton and Lorber (2002) to unknown mint no. 26 in Bactria, related to Ai Khanoum, and dated to the early years of Antiochus' reign. Similar

Fig. 14 | *Tetradrachm minted at Pergamum c. 281–280 BC. Obverse: Head of horned horse. Reverse: Elephant, anchor and BASILEOS SELEU-KOY.*

14 Houghton and Lorber 2002, uncertain mint 18.
15 Mørkholm 1991, 75–6.
16 *Chronographia* 8.202 (http://www.attalus.org/translate/malalas.html).
17 Houghton and Lorber 2002, 469, 471, 472.

silver drachms were minted in the same mint in the name of Antiochus. The motif clearly signifies divine honours. That this was indeed the case is confirmed by inscriptions from Asia Minor (see below). This is not necessarily a specific eastern trait, since we find portraits of Demetrius with bull horns from about 292/291 (see above);[18] these horns have been taken as symbolic of Poseidon, who is depicted on the reverse, or Dionysus. Demetrius included bull's horns in his own portrait in order to signify deification during his lifetime. Horns as a sign of deification were initially depicted on the coins of Ptolemy with the Alexander/Heracles portrait, to which Ammon's horns of a ram were added; these were probably minted after Alexander's corpse had arrived in Egypt.[19] After Ipsus, Lysimachus produced coins of Alexander, not disguised as Heracles, but with beautiful ram horns. Finally, Appian offers a different explanation of why statues of Seleucus included horns:

'He was of such a large and powerful frame that once when a wild bull was brought to sacrifice to Alexander and broke loose from his ropes, Seleucus held him alone, with nothing but his hands, for which reason his statues are ornamented with horns' (Syr.56).

The horned horse head, together with the elephant/elephant quadriga and the anchor clearly acted as the strongest propaganda elements for Seleucus. Of these, the intended meaning of the horned horse head remains enigmatic. It began life as a small symbol but ended up as a significant motif also in the west, as demonstrated by the medallions or coins from Pergamum after the victory at Corupedium.

Antiochus continued to use the horned horse. Thus a series of silver tetradrachms was struck in Sardis with, on the obverse, a portrait of Seleucus with horns, and the horned horse on the reverse. These probably date to shortly after Seleucus' death. Also in the east (Bactria) the horned horse was popular during the reign of Antiochus. Interestingly, gold staters with the horned head of Seleucus and, on the reverse, the horned horse and the inscription *Basileos Seleukou* (but probably minted during the reign of Antiochus), and also very similar staters with the head of the diademed Antiochus and, on the reverse, the horned horse continued to be produced.

---

18 Mørkholm 1991, 79.
19 Mørkholm 1991, 63.

Inscriptions

Benefactions formed an important element of royal ideology, and are best understood from epigraphic evidence; a large portion of the relevant inscriptions have been found in Asia Minor. Characteristic of the interaction between the Greek cities and the Hellenistic kings was the system of euergetism, in which the kings gave rich gifts to the cities; these might have been material gifts and/or promises, such as freedom of the Greek cities.

Antigonus was the Diadoch who established the system of interaction between the Greek cities and the king centred on 'the freedom of the Greek cities'. Two inscriptions from Scepsis dating to 311 (OGIS 5 and 6; translation RC), announcing a letter from Antigonus to the city telling of his success in the agreement with Lysimachus, Cassander and Ptolemy (see chapter 4), deal with the issues of the freedom of the Greeks and peace. It is recorded that 'We have written in the treaty that all Greeks are to swear

Fig. 15 | *The Apollo temple at Didyma. One of the largest Hellenistic temples (51 x 109) built in Ionic style.*

to aid each other in preserving their freedom and autonomy, thinking that, while we lived, in all human expectation these would be protected, but that afterwards freedom would remain more certainly secure for all the Greeks if both they and men in power were bound by oaths.' The answer from Scepsis (OGIS 6) reports that the demos decided to set aside a temenos for Antigonus and make an altar and set up as fine an image as possible, 'and for the sacrifice and the festival to take place in his honour each year, just as it was even formerly carried out; and to crown him with a golden crown of 100 gold [staters]; and to crown also Demetrius and Philip, each with a crown of fifty gold pieces, and to proclaim the crowns [at the] contest during the festival; and for the city to sacrifice [the offering of] glad tidings at the news sent by Antigonus; and for all the citizens to wear garlands, and for the treasurer to provide the expenditure for these things. [Resolved also] to send him gifts of friendship; and to have the agreements and the letters from Antigonus and the oaths which he sent inscribed on a stele, just as Antigonus instructed, and to set it up in the sanctuary of Athena; [and] for the secretary to look after [this]; and for the treasurer to provide the expend-iture for this as well. [Resolved also] for all the citizens to swear the oath that has been sent just as Anti[gonus instructed]; [and] for those chosen'.

Unfortunately, fairly few inscriptions have been found that can inform us about Seleucus' contact with Greek cities or Greek individuals. We have well-preserved inscriptions from Didyma (see below) recording Seleucus and his family as benefactors of the temple of Apollo. The inscriptions also show how contact between the king and a city (or an individual) normally passed through one or more middlemen, either ambassadors or the king's bureaucracy.

Seleucus felt a special affinity towards the sanctuary at Didyma, accord-ing to the Greco-Roman sources. A preserved inscription found in Miletus and dating from 288/287 (Didyma 19; OGIS 214; translation RC 5) records a treasure sent by the king to the Didymaean sanctuary while Poseidippus was stephanephoros and also mentions six men as stewards of the sacred treasures. The inscription contains a detailed list of the dedications:

When Poseidippos was stephanephoros, and the stewards of the sacred treasures were:
Timeas son of Phryson
Aristagoras son of Philemon
Kleomedes son of Kreson
Philippos son of Sosistratos
Alexandros son of Lochegos
Polyxenos son of Babon

Kings Seleucus and Antiochus made the offerings written in this letter.

King Seleucus to the council and the people of Miletus, greetings. We have sent to the sanctuary of the Didymaean Apollo, as offerings to the Saviour Gods, the great lampstand and cups of gold and silver bearing inscriptions; they are under escort of Polianthes. When he comes, then, do you take them, with good fortune, and deposit them in the sanctuary, so that you may use them for libations and other uses on behalf of your health and fortune and the safety of the city for which I wish and you pray. Carry out the written instructions of Polianthes and dedicate the objects sent you and perform the sacrifice, which we have enjoined on him. Aid him in seeing that things are done properly. I have written the list of gold and silver vessels sent to the sanctuary so that you may know the type and the weight of each one. Farewell.

List of gold vessels which were sent:
A phiale of date pattern, inscribed 'of Good Luck (Agathe Tyche)', weight 247 drachmas
Another of date pattern, inscribed 'of Osiris', weight 190 drachmas
Another of date pattern, inscribed 'of Leto', weight 198 drachmas 3 obols
Another of ray pattern, inscribed 'of Hekate', weight 318 drachmas 3 obols
A pair of double deer-head rhytons, inscribed 'of Apollo', weight 318 drachmas 3 obols
Another double deer-head rhyton, inscribed 'of Artemis', weight 161 drachmas
A horn, inscribed 'to Zeus the Saviour', weight 173 drachmas 3 obols
A wine pitcher, inscribed 'of the Saviour Gods', weight 386 drachmas
A barbaric [Persian] wine cooler set with gems, inscribed 'of Soteira', with seven dates missing, weight 372 drachmas
A gold bread-platter, weight 1,088 drachmas
Total weight of gold vessels, weight 3,248 drachmas 3 obols.
A silver cup decorated with figures in relief, with a cord, weight 380 drachmas
A great two-handled wine cooler of silver, weight 9,000 drachmas
Ten talents of frankincense
One talent of myrrh
Two minas of cassia
Two minas of cinnamon
Two minas of costus
A great lamp-stand
He [Polianthes] brought also a sacrifice for the god, 1,000 sheep and 12 steers.

Two further inscriptions from Didyma evidence that Seleucus and his family were honoured there. Thus one inscription[20] concerns a decision to erect a statue of Apame, Seleucus' wife, in the Artemis sanctuary.[21] The inscription is probably to be dated closely after the victory at Ipsus[22] when Seleucus and Antiochus may actually still have been in Asia Minor, possibly accompanied by Apame.

'Resolved by the council and the people, Lycus son of Apollodotus [moved]; concerning the proposal admitted to the council by Demodamas son of [Aristeides], that Apama, wife of king Seleucus, should be honoured, resolved by the council and the people: since Queen Apama / has previously displayed all goodwill and [zeal] for those Milesians who served in the army with [king] Seleucus, and now when [the] ambassadors came [into her presence], whom [king] Seleucus had summoned [from us], she [manifested] no ordinary devotion concerning the construction of the temple of [Apollo] at [Didyma] , / and Antiochus [her son], zealously following the policy of his father Seleucus [over the] sanctuary [at Didyma, has announced] that he would build [a stoa as quickly as possible in the city] … for the god, so that [there might be regular] revenues [from it and that] the sanctuary might be adorned; [resolved by the Milesians: so that] all [may know] / that the people [of Miletus continue to show appropriate care for the benefactors of the people … and the assessors [anataktai] in office after Athenaeus] is crown-bearer of Apollo [should set aside … the money for the [statue from all the sources of the revenue. / This decree is to be inscribed on a stone stele [and placed] in the sanctuary of Artemis at Didyma. The commissioners for the walls [teichopoioi] shall auction the stele and its engraving without exceeding the permitted costs. The treasurers shall provide the cost / from the funds earmarked for the decrees. This decree shall also be inscribed on a whitened board. Comissioners for the (statue): Demodamas son of Aristeides, Lycus son of Apollodotus, Aristophon son of Minnion.'[23]

Antiochus was also clearly active in supporting the sanctuary at Didyma, as noted in the Apame decree and also in a decree dating from about 300/299 (OGIS 213; Didyma 7).

---

20 Austin 2006, no. 51.
21 For the recent find of this sanctuary inside the Apollo sanctuary, see https://www.archaeologie-online.de/blog/lange-gesuchter-tempel-der-artemis-in-didyma-gefunden-2678/
22 See Günther 1971, 25f; Austin 2006, no. 51 dates it to 299/298.
23 Part of the base of the statue may have been found; the base carries an inscription that can be reconstructed as 'queen Apame [object] wife of king Seleucus the people of Miletus [subject] to Artemis in Didyma' (see Tuchelt 1973, 27; Didyma II.113, II.480.21).

'It was resolved by the people, as recommended by the councilors and proposed by Demodamas son of Aristeides: since Antiochus the eldest son of king Seleucus previously has continually shown great goodwill and eagerness concerning the people of Miletus, and now, seeing that his father has [acted] with every concern about the temple at Didyma; and the work completed from [these revenues] will be given by him as offerings to the god; therefore it is resolved by the Milesians to praise [Antiochus] for his piety concerning the god and his goodwill [towards the ? citizens], and to give him land [for the stoa], wherever the appointed architect, along with the men appointed by Antiochus, shall indicate. The treasurers shall sell the land, and the prytaneis in office at the time shall receive the revenue arising from it; they shall keep the money separately, and they shall let out the work to be done, as the people see fit; and when the approved work is completed, it shall be inscribed with "Antiochus the eldest son of Seleucus dedicated this". So that others may choose to show concern for the temple at Didyma and [the populace] of Miletus, seeing that the benefactors [of the temple] are honoured by the people, [it is resolved] by the Milesians to set up [a bronze statue] of Antiochos on horseback, in whatever place [the council] decides to assign; and the Anataktai in office in the year of the stephanephoros [? after Athenaios] shall allocate money for [the statue], whenever they distribute [the other funds]. Antiochus shall be invited [to a privileged seat] in the cyclic chorus contests during the Dionysia [at Miletus] and [the Didymeia] at Didyma. [He] shall be granted [meals] in the prytaneion and freedom from [all] taxes and [security] in peacetime and war, [inviolably and without need for a treaty]. He shall have priority in access to the oracle [in the temple] at Didyma; and the same privileges shall be granted [to the descendants] of Antiochus. So that the statue may be [completed as quickly as possible], the people shall appoint three men [immediately, and they shall] take care of the construction'.

The plan of the stoa clearly shows the importance of the rooms used as shops, while the hall in front is narrow. Coulton compares it with the stoa at Dura Europus and considers it a specific Seleucid design (1977, 89).

To date, a decree concerning honours for Seleucus has not been found, but, from the text of the Apame decree, it must have been the first issued, with those concerning Antiochus and Apame probably following quickly. The Apame decree dedicates many lines to Seleucus' benefaction, which must have been the (re)building of the temple and to the stoa of Antiochus. In contrast, Apame's benefactions are described in more general terms and in a briefer manner; this is probably a question of gender.

The rebuilding of the great temple was not Seleucus' only contribution to the Didymaean sanctuary. He had the old cult statue of Apollo returned to Didyma from the Achaemenid treasury in Susa, just as Alexander had returned the Tyrant Slayers to Athens (Paus. I.16.3, VIII.46.3). The statue was a work of Kanchos of Sikyon and dated from the sixth century BC; it was very similar to the cult statue of Apollo Ismenius in Thebes (Paus. IX.10.2)

Inscriptions from Ilium and Aigai in Aeolis evidence other examples of honours granted to Seleucus – and to Seleucus and Antiochus together – by Greek cities after they had received benefactions from the two kings.

From Ilium, OGIS 212 reads:

'as a friend of the [people of Ilion; and he shall have privileged seating] in the theatre at all [the games that are] held by [our] city; and an altar, [as beautiful as possible], shall be [set up] in the [agora] with the inscription: "of king Seleucus" … [and] the gymnasiarch [shall perform a sacrifice on the altar] on [the twelfth day] of the month in honour of Seleucus, [contests in music], gymnastics and horse-racing; [on the day when the sacrifice] is performed [to Apollo], the founder of his [family], the twelve [tribes] shall go in procession … and there shall be a truce [for the whole month]. The [?] phylarchs shall be given [supplies for the sacrificial offerings, the same] as [they receive] for the [sacrifice] to Athene … on behalf of king [Seleucus] … and the city … in the sacrifice to Athene … the temple wardens (*hieronomoi*), and in the manner that the …'.

An inscription from Aigai (SEG LVIX.1406A)[24] dedicated to both Seleucus and Antiochus following the battle at Corupedium clearly states that the kings were divine:

And good … to Seleucus and Antiochus … so that for all eternity [there may remain the honour awarded(?)] by mankind, the one worthy of their benefactions, with which Seleucus and Antiochos, gods who have manifested themselves, are honoured; moreover, build a most beautiful temple next to the precinct of Apollo and surround it with a free space and dedicate two cult statues as beautiful as possible, having inscribed them with the names of Seleucus and Antiochus, and in front of the temple set up a cult statue and an altar of Soteira; dedicate also an altar opposite the entrance to the temple inscribed "Of Saviours Seleucus and Antiochus"; dedicate also a sacred precinct as beautiful as possible; furthermore, send forth bulls in the hecatomb to the enclosure to Seleucus and Antiochus Saviours, and the women who have allotted shall sacrifice just as to Apollo … and at any rate each month offer two sacrifices on the day we became free; … acts of vehemence[?] … moreover, [divide] the tribes, [however big or small they are], so that

---

24 Malay and Ricl 2009.

there are six instead of four; [name two tribes] Seleucis and Antiochis ... and they themselves and ... and set up in the prytaneion ...

... sacrifice also a bull in the month of Seleuceion just as to Apollo in the month of Thaxios; let also the priest be nominated from all the citizens annually, who will wear a laurel wreath and a headband and a robe as splendid as possible, and together with the [?] authorities at all the sacrifices he will consult the gods, and at the assembly meetings he will begin the sacrifice at the altars of the Saviours, in the same manner as is done to other gods ... the sacred herald at all the sacrifices made at the public cost to the Saviours Seleucus and Antiochus; in the same manner also, when they make drink-offerings before the officials, burn incense and recite vows, and whoever wins the contest of poetry sung to music shall sing a paean over libations; also the prytaneion and the generals' office are to be rebuilt and the prytaneion named Seleucheion and the generals' office Antiocheion. Deliver this decree when the first embassy is dispatched to the king Seleucus and commend him and ask him to preserve his goodwill and friendship, informing him that we shall hand down to posterity the everlasting memory of his benefaction and that we shall make known to all men that we are crowning them with the beautiful crown of glory; engrave this decree on two stelai and set up one of them in Apollo's sanctuary and the other in that of Athene next to the altar of Zeus Saviour; appoint forthwith ten men who will take care of the voted decisions, in order that the decisions are carried out with the outmost speed; the following men were appointed:
Apelles son of Dionysios
Metrobios and Pollichos sons of Athenaios
Athenaios son of Apollodoros
Hyperteros son of Phaitas
Athanos son of Mykkas
Kleomenes son of Hermagoras
Aristogoras son of Athenaios
Apollonides son of Kaikos

Some scholars have concluded that the Seleucus referred to here is Seleucus II, not Seleucus I, mainly because Apollo is mentioned as the founder of the family. Apollo only became the standard figure on Seleucid coins from the time of Antiochus I, but a few such coins were minted already during the lifetime of Seleucus[25], and this may suggest that it is Seleucus I who is referred to. There is also the myth (Pompejus Trogus, Justin 15.4.7–8) that tells how Seleucus' father Antiochus told him, before

---

25   See Ogden 2017, 237.

he left with Alexander, that his real father was actually the god Apollo and that the god had left a ring with a picture of an anchor as a gift to Laodice. It was also told also that Seleucus had a birthmark shaped like an anchor and that Alexander had a similar birthmark, and also his sons and grandsons. This could, of course, be a piece of propaganda invented by Seleucus in order to stress his right to succeed Alexander. Reference is also made to this in a paean to Asclepius from Erythrai, probably dating from 281: 'hymn Seleucus, the child of dark-locked Apollo, whom he of the golden lyre [Apollo again] sired in person [*autos*]'.[26]

A further example of a dedication to both Seleucus and Antiochus is quoted by Athenaeus (VI.254–5) from Phylarchus (Fr. 29), who mentions in his *Histories* that those Athenians who settled in Lemnos were great flatterers. 'For that they, wishing to display their gratitude to the descendants of Seleucus and Antiochus, because Seleucus not only delivered them, when they were severely oppressed by Lysimachus, but also restored both their cities to them, – they, I say, the Athenians in Lemnos, not only erected temples to Seleucus, but also to his son Antiochus; and they have named the cup, which at their feasts is offered at the end of the banquet, the cup of Seleucus the Saviour.'[27] The temples were probably built shortly after the death of Seleucus.

The Seleucid kings learnt to interact in different ways with the various cultures of their empire. Thus, in Babylon there were a range of ethnic groups whom the king addressed in different ways.[28] It is usually assumed, as van der Spek does, that few Greeks lived in Babylon until the time of Antiochus IV. However, in the period under Alexander and Seleucus at least until Seleucia-on-the-Tigris was ready to be occupied, the number of Greeks in the city must have been substantial and they must have formed a specific community, a politeuma or politeia, which had different institutions from those of the Babylonians.[29] The Babylonians were under the authority of the administrative head of the temple and the council of the temple, whereas the Greek community was under the governor of Babylon.[30] The Greek citizens probably met in the theatre (see chapter 8). From

---

26 Ogden 2017, 277.
27 Translation C.D. Yonge https://archive.org/stream/deipnosophistsor01atheuoft/deipnosophistsor01atheuoft_djvu.txt.
28 van der Spek 2009.
29 See Del Monte 1997, 49–52.
30 Specific information related to this derives from the time of Antichos IV, who founded a Greek colony in Babylon (see BCHP https://www.archaeologie-online.de/blog/lange-gesuchter-tempel-der-artemis-in-didyma-gefunden-2678/ According to van der Spek (2001) there was also a community of royal slaves led by 'the prefect of the king'.

the *Astronomical Diaries* it appears that letters from the king were read aloud in the theatre in front of the politai,[31] whereas letters to the Babylonians were read in the Juniper Garden of the Esagila temple.

Antiochus and probably later Seleucid kings seem to some extent to have adapted to Near Eastern traditions when this seemed appropriate, thus clearly acting to maintain the goodwill of the local people. The so-called Antiochus Cylinder, found in the Ezida temple in Borsippa, is undoubtedly a foundation inscription (BM 36277[32]). It has a cuneiform inscription that dates it to 268 and clearly includes propaganda for the king:

Col. I
Antiochos, the great king,
the mighty king, king of the world, king of Babylon, king of [all] countries,
caretaker of Esagila and Ezida,
the [first] bricks
of Esagila and Ezida
in the land of Hatti [= Syria] with my pure hand[s]
I moulded with fine quality oil and
for the laying of the foundation of Ezagila
and Ezida I transported them. In the month of Addaru [XII], on the 20th day,
of the year 43 [Seleukid era = 27 March 268 BC] I laid the foundation of Ezida,
the true temple, the temple of Nabû, which is in Borsippa.
o Nabû, lofty son,
the wise one of the gods, the proud one,
who is eminently worthy of praise,
first born son
Of Marduk, offspring of Erûa,
the queen, who creates offspring,
regard me joyfully, and,
at your lofty command
which is unchanging,
may the overthrow of the country of my enemy,
the achievement of my triumphs,
the predominance over the enemy through victory,
kingship of justice, a reign
of prosperity, years of happiness
[and] the full employment of very old age be the gift.

---

31   van der Spek 2001.
32   Translation see Stol and van der Spek https://www.livius.org/sources/content/ mesopotamian-chronicles-content/antiochus-cylinder/ ; see also Stevens 2014.

Col. II

For the kingship of Antiochus
and king Seleucus, his son,
for ever. O Son of the Prince (Marduk),
offspring of queen Erûa:
at your entry into Ezida, the true house,
the house of your Anu-ship, the dwelling of your heart's desire,
with rejoicing and jubilation,
may – at your true command,
which cannot be annulled – my days be long,
my years many,
my throne firm,
my reign long lasting on your sublime writing board
Which sets the boundary of heaven and earth.
May my good [fate] constantly be established in your pure mouth,
may my hands conquer the countries from sunrise
to sunset,
that I might inventory their tribute
and bring it to make perfect Esagila and Ezida. O Nabû,
foremost son, when you enter Ezida,
the true house,
may good [fate] for Antiochus, king of all countries,
king Seleucus, his son,
[and] Stratonike,
his consort, the queen, may their good [fate]
be established by your command [*lit*: in/by your mouth].

Two Babylonian tablets offer us glimpses of other aspects of Antiochus' attitude towards Babylonian religion. BCHP 5 tells of Antiochus and the temple of Sin (the moon god), where Antiochus, as crown prince, is instructed by a Babylonian (priest?) to perform offerings to Sin. 'He prostrated himself and provided one sheep for offering'. To prostrate oneself for a god is a Babylonian, not a Greek custom. On the reverse, a central part of the text records how Antiochus settled the Macedonians, 'as many as there were in Babylon', from Babylon to Seleucia.

Tablet BCHP 6 describes how the crown prince (Antiochus) gave an offering at the ruins of the Esagila, and fell on the ruins. He made an offering in Greek fashion, and his troops, wagons and elephants removed the debris of the Esagila. It seems that Antiochus was accustomed to Greek ways, and had to be instructed in Babylonian customs when sacrificing to Sin.

Seleucus probably would not have behaved in the same way; he always saw himself as a Macedonian, as is also stressed in this inscription and in particular in BCHP 9, where he declares that he is going home to Macedonia (see chapter 5). But, on the other hand we know that he permitted local populations to continue their own religious traditions, and apparently made no attempt to change them.

CHAPTER 8

The coloniser

Seleucus followed Alexander in founding a large number of settlements throughout his realm; in fact, of the Diadochs, he became the coloniser *par excellence*. Huge numbers of settlers were essential for the upkeep of the enormous empire and to maintain his military power. The enormous colonisation project clearly demanded land for the settlement of the colonists and thus often necessitated the relocation of local populations.

According to Appian (*Syr.* 57), Seleucus founded 16 Antiochs, five Laodicaeas, nine Seleucias, three Apameas and one Stratonicaea, and also more than 20 cities that he named after Macedonian/Greek cities. The colonial settlements varied in terms of scale from fortresses to small towns and large cities; some grew to become exceptionally large.[1] These efforts were continued by Seleucus' son and other successors. It is important to acknowledge that the dating of material culture can rarely be as precise as that of political history (see also Introduction). Thus, I have in this chapter taken a broader perspective, though attempting as far as possible to concentrate on the period of Seleucus and Antiochus or, on occasion, the early Seleucid period in general.

At Triparadeisus, where Seleucus was appointed satrap of Babylonia, he gained not only a fertile province but also the city of Babylon, which had been Alexander's administrative centre for the eastern part of his empire.[2] Babylon's political role had, of course, diminished as the focus of the rivalry between the Diadochs moved west in the years following Alexander's death, and two satraps had governed Babylonia in the period between Alexander's death and the events at Triparadeisus (see chapters 2 and 3). Geographically, Babylonia bound together the western and eastern

---

1   Cohen 2013.
2   Capdetrey 2007, 31, n. 35.

parts of Alexander's empire and this role continued. Babylon, however, was not the only centre of the region. Thus Susa, where the eastern satraps gathered at the beginning of the campaign between Eumenes and Antigonus (see chapter 3), with its treasury, remained important, as was Ecbatana in Media; it was these two cities that Seleucus chose as the locations of important mints following the Babylonian War. Further east, Alexander had founded several cities in Bactria, and colonists – many of them probably soldiers or veterans – had been settled by him in these cities. That settlement in such distant lands did not always create satisfied settlers is evidenced by the revolt in Bactria following Alexander's death, which Peithon suppressed (see chapter 2).

Kings as city founders

Colonisation must have required royal attention and power, and this is attested by a decree inscription found in Magnesia-on-the-Meander that was sent from Antioch in Persis.[3] The decree is a positive answer to Magnesia, who had sent ambassadors to many cities, including Antioch-Persis,[4] asking them to contribute to and participate in a festival that the city intended to initiate for Artemis Leucophryne. The decree is from the time of Antiochus III and his son, and concerns the festival and the despatch of ambassadors to Magnesia. It includes the following passage:

'In the year in which the priest of Seleucus Nicator and of Antiochus Soter and of Antiochus Theos and of Seleucus Callinicus and of King Antiochus [III] and of the son of King Antiochus was Heracleitus, the son of Zoes, first six-month period [period of office], decisions of the main assembly, which was recorded by Asclepiades, the son of Hecataeus, the son of Demetrius, the secretary of the Council and the People, month Pantheos, third day before the end of the month; resolved by the assembly on the motion of the prytaneis. The people of Magnesia-on-the-Maeander are kinsmen and friends of our people [demos of Antioch-Persis] and have performed many distinguished services for the Greeks [which] relate [to glory]. Formerly, when Antiochus Soter [I] was eager to increase our city, as it was called after him, and sent [an embassy] about [the sending of] a colony, they passed an honourable and glorious decree, offered a sacrifice and sent a sufficient number

---

3   Austin 2006, no. 190 = OGIS 233.
4   Similar decrees were also issued by Seleucia-on-the-Tigris, Apamea near the river Sellas, Seleucia by the Red Sea, Seleuca by the Eulaos (Susa), Seleuca ..., Antioch ... and Alexandria ... (this part of the stele is damaged).

of men of great personal excellence, as they were eager to help in increasing the people of Antioch.'

As Austin comments, the king had clearly been putting pressure on Magnesia. The decree was brought to Magnesia by ambassadors who had travelled approximately 2,000 km between the two cities. The fact that travelling such distances was undertaken quite often by all kinds of people, and that ancient roads were often busy, is frequently overlooked; we often forget that until very recent times travelling conditions had remained similar for thousands of years, and did not prevent people from undertaking such journeys.[5]

Prior to Ipsus, Seleucus' focus was on Babylonia, with its fertile land, and his colonisation efforts were mainly concentrated on the middle and lower Tigris region. Following the victory at Ipsus, his attention shifted to northern Syria.

All the kings, apart from Ptolemy, built new capitals in their own names.[6] Perhaps the best description of these royal undertakings, clearly emulating Alexander's many Alexandrias, is Hieronymus' record of Antigonus' building of Antigoneia in Syria (see chapter 3). Thus, Seleucus' initial capital, Babylon, was soon replaced by Seleucia-on-the-Tigris.

Seleucia-on-the-Tigris

The choice of Babylonia as the region in which Seleucus built his first capital clearly points to his perception of Babylonia as the heartland of his kingdom in the period before Ipsus (301). To him, this was his spear-won land following the Babylonian War. The decision to move the administrative centre from Babylon to a new city was undoubtedly primarily undertaken for ideological reasons. Seleucia must, of course, have been built

---

5   One such example from the first half of the 19th century is a Danish nobleman, Count Preben Bille Brahe, who every year travelled to Rome with his horse-drawn carriages, a distance of c. 2000 km (see Højrup 1982, 204).

6   Thus Antigonus chose to found Antigoneia in Syria. Syria was well chosen with easy access not only to the Mediterranean but also overland to Asia Minor, Babylonia and, not least, south where an army could quickly march against Ptolemy in Egypt. The building of the city probably began after Antigonus had appointed himself king. From Diodorus Siculus (XX.47.5) we learn that the foundation was initiated in 307, and that it was laid out 'on a lavish scale, making its perimeter seventy stades; for the location was well adapted for watching over Babylon and the upper satrapies, and again for keeping an eye upon lower Syria and the satrapies near Egypt'. In 'Europe', Lysimachus had already built a city carrying his name, Lysimachaea, in 309.

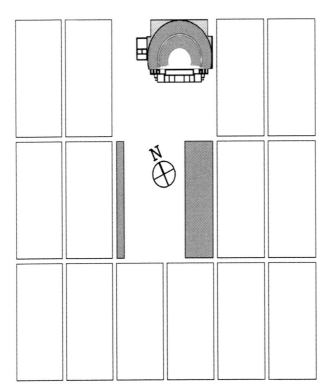

Fig. 16 | *Plan of North Agora in Seleucia-on-the-Tigris.*

after the Babylonian War, i.e. after 308, and undoubtedly before 301.[7] In some cuneiform texts it is referred to as a royal city.[8]

For his new capital, Seleucus chose a location adjacent to Opis, on the west bank of the Tigris. This was a city that dated back to the Bronze Age and it was an ancient emporion on the east-west route about 60 km north of Babylon (c. 30 km south of modern-day Baghdad). The lower part of the Tigris had been made navigable by Alexander after removal of the weirs that the Achaemenid administration had built to facilitate irrigation; this made connections with the Persian Gulf and Susa much easier.[9] Now, a royal canal was constructed, linking the Tigris with the Euphrates so that western Babylonia was also easily reached from the new capital, and large harbour structures were built. The royal canal made access to the west easy, whilst the Diyala valley led up to the Iranian plateau to Ecbatana

7   See Kosmin 2014, 187; Cohen 2013, 157, n. 2 with several references.
8   Cohen 2013, 157 n. 3. This probably meant simply that it was one of the cities in which the court some-times stayed (Kosmin 2014, 143-151).
9   See Kosmin 2014, 187.

CHAPTER 8   114

from where the highway continued to Bactria. The site was thus well chosen, as one would expect from Seleucus, who was by now very familiar with the terrain of this part of his empire.

According to Strabo (XVI.1.5), Seleucus fortified the new city and transferred the basileion to it from Babylon. Pausanias (I.16.3) records that the king brought colonists from Babylon to Seleucia. BCHP 5[10] notes that Seleucus' co-regent, Antiochus, settled Macedonians, as many as there were in Babylon, in Seleucia. Quite a significant number of Macedonians and Greeks must by this time have been living in Babylon. According to Pliny (*HN* VI.122), the walls of Seleucia formed the shape of an eagle spreading its wings, and the city had in his time 600,000 inhabitants. Approximately 550 hectares seem to have been encompassed within the walls. Appian (*Syr.* 58) tells us that the magi resisted the building of the new city. However, Babylon was in no way deserted and continued to operate as an important religious centre, as the construction of temples attests (see chapters 7 and 9). A group of Greek administrators and sufficient military personnel to control any local unrest must have remained in Babylon.

Despite two extensive excavation campaigns (an American one in 1927–37 and an Italian one in 1964–76 and 1986–9), Hellenistic Seleucia is still not well understood, largely due to the extensive Parthian layers.[11] No more than about 5% of the city has been excavated and little of it down to the Seleucid level(s). However, it is clear that the city was laid out in the Greek fashion, with a grid plan, with house blocks of no less than approximately 140 x 70 m. A large canal supplied with water from the Tigris flowed east-west and thus divided the city in half. Large unoccupied spaces suggest several agoras. The northern agora, situated to the north of the city and in the centre of the grid, is the best known in terms of the Seleucid period (the layers of which proved extremely difficult to reach for both expeditions, due to the high water-table). We do not know for certain what portion of the city dates back to the time of Seleucus, but it must presumably be most if not all of the city plan and the walls, though these may have altered several times.

The largest tell, Tell 'Umar, now measuring 13 m in height and 94 x 76 m at its base, is located on the northern side of the city and was identified by the American expedition as a ziggurat. However, the Italian expedition, which reached the Seleucid levels, concluded that it is the remains of a

---

10 https://www.livius.org/sources/content/mesopotamian-chronicles-content/
bchp-5-antiochus-i-and-sin-temple-chronicle/
See van der Spek and Finkel.

11 Messina 2011.

theatre.[12] A small building next to it may be a temple in Mesopotamian style.[13] On the western side of the agora, the Italian team excavated a very large Seleucid building, covering no less than 2600 m². This was identified as an archive since it contained more than 25,000 clay seal impressions. The building was about 140 m long and the documents were placed inside on wooden shelves set in niches (see also chapter 9). The building burnt down after 129 BC, according to the date of the latest seal impression (see chapter 9). A large number of the documents relate to the payment of salt taxes. Standing opposite the archive, a stoa of at least 40 m in length also dates back to the Seleucid period.[14] The construction material of the walls of these buildings is mudbrick or baked brick, in the old Mesopotamian tradition. Undoubtedly, from its early phase, Seleucia also housed temples, probably in both Greek and Mesopotamian styles, one or more gymnasia and a basileion, which may have been situated south of the canal.

The growth of the population in the area of the new capital and Babylon must have depended on significantly increasing the yield of barley and other agricultural products from, for example, the Diyala plain between the Tigris and the Zagros mountains[15], as well as other areas.[16] Survey work in the Diyala valley has enabled Adams to demonstrate intense growth of villages and farmsteads in the valley at this time (1965; see van der Spek 2007, 39 for a table summarising Adams' results); a similar picture is attested in western Syria (see below). Van der Spek has tentatively concluded that the Diyala valley could produce sufficient grain to support the large population of the city (2007, 41). Taking the current irrigated area of the valley as his starting point,[17] he estimates that, with a yield of 2,000 litres per hectare, the area can produce 1,074,000,000 litres (665,800 tonnes) of barley per annum. Thus, with an estimated requirement of 250 kg per person per year, in normal years the area could feed about 2.5 million people.

Ai Khanoum

Alexander had founded or refounded a number of cities in Bactria[18] and settled soldiers and veterans in them; Seleucus probably continued this practice. One large city, Ai Khanoum (Greek name unknown) in eastern

Fig. 17 | *Plan of Ai Khanoum.*

---

12 Invernizzi 1990; 1994; Messina 2011.
13 Messina 2011.
14 Messina 2017, fig. 2.5
15 Adams 1965.
16 van der Spek 2007.
17 Adams 1965, 23.
18 See Cohen 2013.

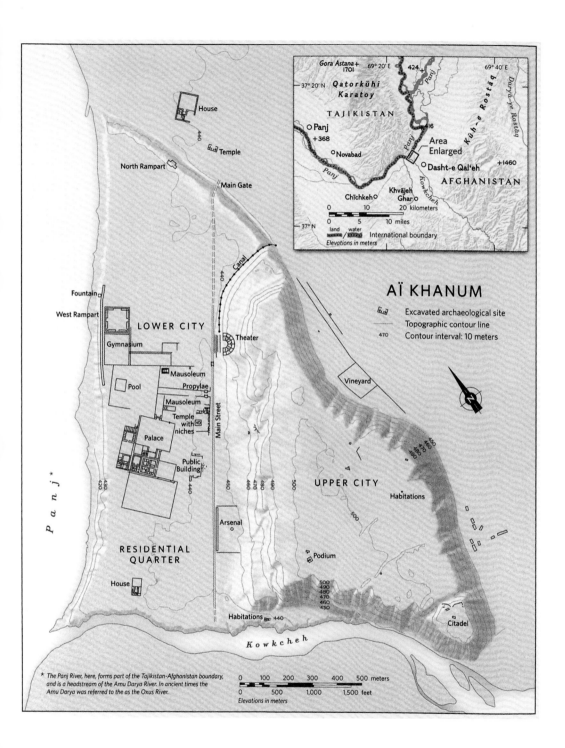

AÏ KHANUM

House

Temple

North Rampart

Main Gate

Canal

Fountain

West Rampart

LOWER CITY

Gymnasium

Theater

Mausoleum

Pool

Propylae

Mausoleum

Temple with niches

Palace

Public Building

Main Street

Arsenal

RESIDENTIAL QUARTER

House

Habitations

Kowkcheh

Vineyard

UPPER CITY

Habitations

Podium

Citadel

P a n j ⭑

N

Excavated archaeological site

Topographic contour line

470   Contour interval: 10 meters

Inset map:

Gora Astana+ 1701   69° 20' E   424 +   Panj   69° 40' E

37° 20' N

Qatorkŭhi Karatoy

TAJIKISTAN

Panj
+368

Novabad

416

Area Enlarged

Dasht-e Qal'eh

Kŭh-e Rostāq

Darya-ye Rostāq

+1460

AFGHANISTAN

Chīchkeh

Khvājeh Ghar

0   10   20 kilometers

0   5   10 miles

37° N

land   water   International boundary

Elevations in meters

* The Panj River, here, forms part of the Tajikistan-Afghanistan boundary, and is a headstream of the Amu Darya River. In ancient times the Amu Darya was referred to the as the Oxus River.

0   100   200   300   400   500 meters

0   500   1,000   1,500 feet

Elevations in meters

Bactria, at the confluence of the Oxus and the Kochka rivers, was excavated by a French expedition between 1965 and 1978. The city is situated on a fertile plain, which revealed evidence of an irrigation system dating back to the Bronze Age. The excavators initially dated the founding of the city to the late fourth century or around 300 BC.[19] Recently, however, many scholars have lowered the foundation date to the reign of Antiochus I.[20] However, it seems more likely that the city was founded either by Alexander or, most probably, by Seleucus, and that building was continued by Antiochus I. This city may possibly be identified with a city recorded in the texts as Eucratidaea, and thus renamed by one of the independent Greco-Bactrian kings, Eucratides (I). Prior to the foundation of the city, a number of Achaemenid settlements existed on the plain; they now fell into ruin or were simply erased, such as the fortress at Kohna Qala close to Ai Khanoum.[21]

The city's water supply came not directly from the rivers but from a branch of the irrigation canals that ran between the main street and the foot of the acropolis. As seen later in the large Syrian cities and probably also in Seleucia-on-the-Tigris, the layout is characterised by a long central street, of no less than 1.5 km in length; this seems to be a specific trait of the major Seleucid cities. An aerial photograph of the southern portion of the city shows part of the grid plan of the streets.[22] The city housed two of the most characteristic structures of Greek Hellenistic urban culture: a gymnasium[23] and a theatre.[24] The building material is principally traditional local mudbrick. Among the first constructions must have been the wall, fortified with rectangular towers, which surrounded the city and the citadel on the acropolis. Furthermore, the central street, the heroon of Kineas (see below) and the main temple must also belong to the first period of the settlement. The excavated palace and many other buildings probably belong to the period of the Greco-Bactrian kings. However, a palace probably also existed during the early period. An agora has not been found, so far, but the large courtyard of the palace may have functioned as such. The excavated gymnasium[25] had a predecessor, as too did the theatre in all likelihood.

19 Bernard 2008.
20 See, e.g., Martinez-Sève 2014.
21 Gardin 1998.
22 Martinez-Sève 2014, 276, fig. 8.
23 Veuve 1987.
24 Bernard 1978, 429–41.
25 Veuve 1987.

Northern Syria

After the victory at Ipsus, Seleucus threw his energy as a coloniser into his new territory in northern Syria, where, across the area called Seleukis, he is linked to at least four large cities known collectively as the Tetrapolis: Seleucia Pieria, Antioch-on-the-Orontes, Laodicaea ad mare and Apamea. The victory at Ipsus offered him the opportunity to transform this landscape, which seems mainly to have been occupied by rural settlements in the Achaemenid period, along with possibly a number of very large estates owned by the Persian elite.[26] Probably already under Persian rule the age-old city of Ebla and settlements on other Bronze Age tells reduced in size.[27] From the Seleucid conquest onwards, areas such as the Amuq plain and the surrounding highlands witnessed an expansion in the number of settlements, a pattern that can be traced from the early Hellenistic into the later Hellenistic period and on into the Roman, culminating in the late Roman period.[28] Antigonus had earlier founded a city here in his own name – Antigoneia (Diod. Sic. XX.47.5–6; Strabo XVI.2.4; Livy XLIV.10) – but Seleucus founded no less than the four large cities of the Tetrapolis, all named after himself and his family, together with a number of smaller towns and fortresses. This significant effort clearly bears witness to the fact that, by this time, not only did Seleucus control enormous resources but also that he wanted this part of his empire to become at least as important as Babylonia, and probably more so. A consequence of his pragmatic approach to keeping together his enormous realm was the appointment of his son, Antiochus, as co-regent in 294, with a centre in Babylon. Father and son seem to have worked well together, with Seleucus undoubtedly the final decision-maker.

Since he was later buried there, Seleucia (in Pieria), bearing the king's own name, was clearly chosen by Seleucus as his western capital. It was here that Seleucus marked his final victory over Antigonus by dismantling Antigoneia and having the building materials transported to Seleucia. The

---

26 Hannestad 2013.

27 There is dispute among archaeologists as to whether there really was a hiatus of occupation at many sites or even across whole regions or whether this only appears to be the case because diagnostic material from the Persian period has not yet been identified. Thus Wilkinson (2004) suggests that Persian material culture may actually have been a continuation of earlier local culture(s), in contrast to that of the Seleucid period, which is easy to identify due to the Seleucids' 'conspicuous material assemblage'. However, the fact that further south, on the coast of Phoenicia and in Palestine, archaeological material from the Persian period is rich and easily recognised rather supports the view that during the Persian period Syria was a mainly rural and sparsely populated region (Hannestad 2013).

28 Wilkinson 2003.

inhabitants of Antigoneia were also probably transferred to the new city (Diod. Sic. XX.47.9), although Strabo (XVI.2.4), Libanius (*Or.* XI.92) and Iohannes Malalas (VIII.201) record that the inhabitants of Antigoneia were transferred to Antioch. Seleucia was situated on the southern slopes of the Amanus mountain range, and Polybius offers us the following description of the city at the time of Antiochus III, following his regaining of the city from the Ptolemies in 219 BC.

'The situation of Seleucia and the nature of its surroundings are as follows. It lies on the sea between Cilicia and Phoenicia, and above it rises a very high mountain called Coryphaeum, washed on its western side by the extreme waters of the sea separating Cyprus from Phoenicia, but overlooking with its eastern slopes the territories of Antioch and Seleucia. Seleucia lies on its southern slope, separated from it by a deep and difficult ravine. The town descends in a series of broken terraces to the sea, and is surrounded on most sides by cliffs and precipitous rocks. On the level ground at the foot of the slope which descends towards the sea lies the business quarters (emporia) and a suburb defended by very strong walls. The whole of the main city is similarly fortified by walls of very costly construction and is splendidly adorned with temples and other fine buildings. On the side looking to the sea it can only by approached by a flight of steps cut in the rock with frequent turns and twists all the way up' (Polybius V.59.3).[29]

According to Polybius, the city had no more than 6,000 free inhabitants and Antiochus III allowed those who had been in exile to return to the city. Though 'free inhabitants' probably refers to free males only, this figure still signifies a fairly small total number of inhabitants. By this time, the population of Antioch (see below) probably far outnumbered that of Seleucia, which, as noted above, must have been Seleucus' western capital. The American expedition that worked in Antioch and Seleucia in the 1930s discovered a peripteral Doric temple which probably had 6 x 12 columns,[30] and I have suggested elsewhere that this was the burial place of Seleucus, the so-called Nicotoreion.[31] In addition, approximately 5 km of the walls, including nine towers and the staircase mentioned by Polybius, have been found.

Antioch-on-the-Orontes (modern-day Antakya in Turkey) became the western capital at least from the reign of Antiochus I. Unfortunately, very

---

29 H.J. Edwards see http://penelope.uchicago.edu/Thayer/E/Roman/Texts/Polybius/home.html
30 Stillwell 1941, 33–4.
31 Hannestad and Potts 1990.

little archaeological evidence from the Hellenistic period has been found and the literary sources date mainly from Late Antiquity. Strabo, one of the earlier sources, calls the city in itself a Tetrapolis, 'since it consists of four parts: and each of the four settlements is fortified both by a common wall and a wall of its own. Now Nikator founded the first of the settlements, transferring thither the settlers from Antigoneia, which had been built near it a short time before by Antigonus; the second was founded by a multitude of settlers; the third (the palace area) by Seleucus Callinicus; and the fourth by Antiochus Epiphanes' (XV.2.4). Antioch grew to become the second-largest city in the eastern Mediterranean after Alexandria. Although very little is known of the city in the Hellenistic period, it seems that its layout was, in many ways, similar to that of Seleucia-on-the-Tigris. From its foundation, the city seems to have had a long central street running between the river and the mountain slopes (probably largely identical with the modern main street). The layout was based on a grid plan.[32] The finds of black-glazed pottery, particularly in the northern part of the later Roman city, may suggest that the earliest part of Antioch was situated here.[33] As to the complex construction of the city walls, the earliest portion was built in a kind of polygonal technique.[34] Finally, the rivers crossing the region made it easy to transport food and other resources to Antioch. The development here seems to be very similar to that noted above for the Diyala valley.[35]

Apamea, situated inland on the bank of the Orontes, was named after Seleucus' wife. According to Strabo, the city was well fortified and beautifully situated on a hill – with the acropolis located on a second hill – surrounded by plains and marshes (XVI.2.10). The conditions here were perfect for the pasturing of cattle and horses, and the main stabling for Seleucus' elephants was also located here. The city had had two names before Apamea; the first, Pharnake, suggests an Achaemenid settlement, whilst the second, Pella, was, according to Strabo (XVI.2.10), adopted when the city was refounded by the first Macedonians. Very little from the Hellenistic period has been preserved, probably due to a destructive earthquake in AD 115. Nonetheless, it seems that during this period the city had two phases, with the first relating to the foundation of the city.[36] A lamp found in the foundation of the wall indicates that its construction should

---

32 For a discussion of the many suggestions regarding the layout of the city, see Hannestad 2013; De Giorgi 2016.

33 De Giorgi 2016.

34 Hannestad 2013, 258; De Giorgi 2016, 58ff.

35 Hannestad 2013; de Giorgio 2016.

36 Leriche 1987; Balty 2003.

be dated to the period of either Antigonus or Seleucus. Lamps – probably Attic imports – of Howland's type 25A–D[37] evidence very early Hellenistic occupation in most parts of the city. The walls encompassed an area of approximately 255 hectares.[38] Laodicaea ad mare is described by Strabo (XVI.2.9) as a beautifully built city with a good harbour. The modern street grid is apparently based on the original layout of the city with the typical central street.[39] In Seleucus' lifetime this was the largest mint in Syria, possibly targeted at the international market.[40]

Seleucus, or his immediate successors, also founded a number of smaller cities at strategic points in the region in order to control the area and secure the overland routes to the Euphrates. At this period there seem to have been two overland routes towards the northern crossing of the Euphrates at Zeugma.[41] Some of the settlements were much older and simply refoundations given new Macedonian or Greek names. Characteristic of such cases is that a new orthogonal street plan was constructed on top of the layout of the old settlement. Travelling from Antioch on one of these routes, a convenient resting place would be Gindaros in the valley of the Afrin river, and an orthogonal street grid has been detected on the largest tell in the area.[42] The tell is eroded and thus it is not possible to determine whether it was fortified. The pottery recovered includes a significant amount of black-glazed ware, some probably imported but most from Antioch. The ceramic assemblage also includes Hellenistic amphorae, mainly Rhodian (as is the case across the eastern Mediterranean), of which a few are of third-century date, whilst most date to the first half of the second century. Habitation of the settlement continued through the Roman period and into the early Byzantine. The oldest coins found at the site are from Seleucus' time, dating from the 280s.

Further along the northern route (about 100 km from Antioch), Cyrrhus should probably also be counted among Seleucus' foundations. The site includes a distinct and easily defensible acropolis and remained in use into the Byzantine period. Stretches of the wall are built in a polygonal technique, and these sections are probably remnants of the first wall. The streets were laid out in a grid with the main street running north-south.[43]

37 Howland 1958.
38 Balty 2000.
39 Sauvaget 1934 and 1936.
40 Houghton and Lorber 2002, 25.
41 Comfort, Abadie-Renal and Ergec 2000.
42 Kramer 2004.
43 https://journals.openedition.org/archeosciences/1584.

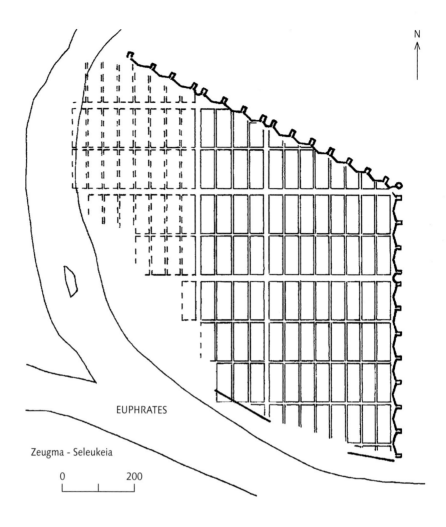

Fig. 18 | *Plan of Apamea-on-the-Orontes.*

N

EUPHRATES

Zeugma - Seleukeia

0   200

Along the Euphrates

Along the Euphrates, a number of fortified settlements were founded to control and probably also protect traffic on the river. On the eastern bank, geophysical surveys and excavations have offered insight into the history and layout of Apamea-on-the-Orontes.[44] Three sides of the city wall surround an area of approximately 40 hectares, while the fourth side runs along the river. The wall was built in a polygonal technique, with the upper part constructed of mudbrick. The grid plan of the city is very well attested. Those streets leading to the gates are wider (c. 10 m) than the others, and the insulae are about 105 m long and 38 m wide. The pottery

---

44 Desmenaux et al. 1999; Abbadie-Reynal and Gaborit 2003.

from the uppermost floors of the excavated shops and houses, including black-glazed wares and early shapes of Eastern Sigillata A, suggests that the site was destroyed around the middle of the second century BC. A burnt layer covers the site.

On the western side of the Euphrates, on a rock overlooking the river, sits the city of Jebel Khalid. This was excavated by an Australian team from the mid-1980s until 2010, and, from a Seleucid perspective, is probably the most interesting site excavated in Syria. It was founded around 300, or in the first quarter of the third century, and was abandoned before the end of the Hellenistic period.[45] Thus Jebel Khalid presents an exclusively Seleucid settlement. A wall protected the inland side and the southern river front-age, whilst the acropolis had a separate inner wall. The outer wall included some 30 towers and bastions, and covered an area of about 50 hectares. According to the excavator, a massive gate complex was built in the first half of the third century,[46] but it may actually be later since the ceramics from the construction level suggest a date not earlier than the last quarter of the third century.[47] A structure that has been identified as the governor's palace is situated on the acropolis, and this probably dates to the first half of the third century. Luxurious decoration characterises a large room on its northern sides (see chapter 9 fig. 33). Between the palace in the south and a housing area in the north, excavations have also revealed remains of a Doric temple (see chapter 9).[48] The excavated housing quarter[49] contained insulae measuring 90 m north-south and 35 m east-west. The structures here offer an interesting insight into the house types of the Seleukid colonies. Little is known of the street grid; although it does seem that the streets running north-south were broader than those running east-west, as was the case in many Greek cities.

About 100 km south of Jebel Khalid, the city of Europus (Dura Europus) was also founded by Seleucus. The city continued to flourish during Roman and Parthian times, and, to a significant extent, the later city hid or destroyed earlier buildings. Nevertheless, following its excavation in 1922–3 and 1928–37 it was considered a model Seleucid colony. In recent years, however, our understanding of the Hellenistic city – with an orthogonal street plan and a main street running northeast-southwest as part of the

---

45 The earliest coins are two posthumous Alexander silver coins and two bronzes of Seleucus; the latest Hellenistic examples date from the late 70s BC (Nixon 2002).

46 Clarke 2002a.

47 See also Berlin 2003.

48 Clarke 2005.

49 Jackson 2014.

Fig. 19 | *View of Jebel Khalid and the Euphrates.*

original settlement – has been challenged by Leriche (1987; 2003; 2004; 2007; Leriche and Gelin 1997). Leriche concludes that early Dura Europus consisted of the citadel and the area around it only, with access through a wadi to the river bank, and that the rest of the city belongs to the second century BC. These arguments are, in my opinion, not entirely convincing,[50] and the extent of the outer wall, with a gate towards the west, encompassing approximately 63 hectares, actually fits well with that of Jebel Khalid. This does not mean, of course, that the whole city was built before the death of Seleucus, just the initial part. Thus Hopkins notes that Hellenistic coins are a rarity, except from the vicinity of the redoubt (strategeion) and citadel.[51] One may surmise that, when the redoubt and the citadel were built, the first settlement clustered near the River Gate and below on the river plain. Furthermore, finds of early Hellenistic lamps seem to concen-

50 Hannestad 2013.
51 Hopkins 1979, 255.

trate at the citadel and around the strategeion.[52] The numismatic evidence from Dura Europos does indeed indicate strong activity already under Antiochus I (89 coins) and Seleucus II (80 coins).[53]

Asia Minor

For a few months at the very end of his reign, Seleucus' capital in Asia Minor was Sardis, the old capital of the Lydians and an important satrapal seat of the Achemenids. The Royal Road from Susa to Sardis became the principal highway of Seleucus' empire after Corupedium.

Thus, the intensive programme of founding new cities and refounding old ones begun in Asia Minor during the time of Alexander was continued by the Diadochs. Seleucid control of large parts of the region after Corupedium led to there being no break in this activity. There are significant numbers of Seleucias, Antiochias and foundations with other names clearly connected with Seleucus and his successors to be found in the literary and epigraphical sources.[54] Seleucus and his immediate successors were very active in founding settlements in the interior of Asia Minor, particularly on or near trade routes connecting the Aegean coast with the east. The land routes were particularly important because of the relative weakness of the Seleucid fleet compared with the Ptolemaic one. The most important road, apart from the Royal Road, was a more southerly route, called the Common Road by Strabo (14.2.29), that ran through the Meander valley and was used by those travelling from Ephesus; in Hellenistic times it became the main trade route across Asia Minor. Settlements and fortresses were built to protect the Common Road against threats from the mountain peoples to the south (Pisidians and Isaurians), and a number of settlements in the region are known.[55]

Olba, approximately 20 km from the coast, was, at least for a period, under the control of Seleucus, who contributed to the building of the important sanctuary of Zeus Olbios. An inscription tells us that he built the stoa at the west end of the temple. The date of the temple itself (in Corinthian style) has been much discussed, and in more recent years considered

---

52 Baur 1947.
53 And, of course, under Antiochus III, whose coins show peaks across the empire, and Seleucus III (80 coins). Later, there is a small peak under Antichos VII (62 coins). This pattern does not correspond to Leriche's dating of the walls and layout of the city (for similar reflections, see also Yon 2003).
54 Cohen 1996.
55 Grainger 1990, 185.

later, probably from the time of Antiochus. However, one would assume that Seleucus would rather have built or restored the temple also.

A different type of settlement from those mentioned so far is an enormous fortress which has only become known in recent years. It is situated in north eastern Cilicia on Mount Karasis, at a height of about 900–1050 m, and consists of a lower and an upper fortress and a large courtyard (see Radt 2011). In the upper fortress two buildings, probably used as a banquet hall and a residence building for the officer who was in charge of the fortress, were situated. The complex is difficult to access from all sides and cannot have been intended as the acropolis of a planned city. A relief showing an elephant on one of the walls clearly marks it as a Seleucid fortress. It is indeed the best-preserved fortress from the period, but unfortunately it has not been possible to excavate on the site. Thus so far the date depends on surveys and studies of the building technique of the walls. Radt (2011) has used the Megarian sherds as an indicator that the fortress may have been built by Antiochus IV. The elephant emblem would rather suggest Seleucus I, Antiochus I or Antiochus III, who all made an anabasis to the east. The find of Megarian bowls of course indicates that the fortress was in use in the early second century BC. However, it must remain uncertain when the fortress was first built. The fertile plain of Cilicia was highly important, often used for wintering of armies during the time of Alexander, Antigonus and Seleucus. It has been speculated that the complex might be identified as Cyinda, the most important treasury in eastern Asia Minor. Without excavations on the site, the dating of the complex is not possible.

Together with the colonial cities, such fortresses – probably mainly smaller than this – characterized the enormous empire that Seleucus created.

CHAPTER 9

From palaces to pottery: material culture in the Seleucid realm

In this chapter, aspects of material culture will be used to examine how such an enormous realm and its various regions and their cultures responded to the changing world after the conquest of Alexander and the formation of the Seleucid Empire, from royal palaces to more humble objects such as pottery and terracottas. As already stressed in the Introduction and chapter 8, dating of material culture is often only possible within a fairly broad time frame. Assigning a precise date to the reign of Seleucus is rarely possible, except for coins, which are discussed in chapters 6 and 7.

Babylonia

Excavations and other forms of research have been conducted in the region of Babylonia for more than a century. And, though scholarly interest has mainly concentrated on earlier periods, there has been a change of emphasis over time, at least since the 1930s. We are now able to study the material culture from three different types of cities: (1) a new foundation, Seleucia-on-the-Tigris, the new capital referred to as a royal city; (2) the old capital of the region, Babylon; and (3) an old city, Uruk, which is particularly famous for its temples and where studies in astronomy and astrology played an important role.

Uruk

More than a century of excavations, conducted by German teams, have taken place at Uruk and have revealed what is so far the most complete example of a Babylonian city during Seleucid times.[1] The years between about 300 and 125 BC seem to have been the most intensive building

---

1   Falkenstein 1941; Finkbeiner 1993; Boehmer et al. 1995; Kose and Bartel 1998; Lindström 2003.

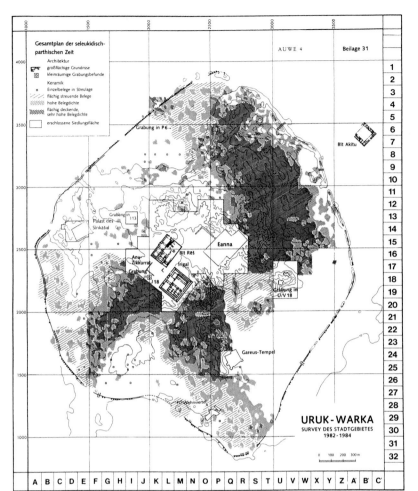

Fig. 20 | *Plan of Uruk from the Hellenistic period.*

period in the history of the city, which by that time covered approximately 300 hectares. The kings of the early Seleucid period, possible beginning with Antiochus I, were directly or indirectly involved in the building of two large temples – the Bit Res sanctuary and the Irigal – along with the largest-known ziggurat. The layouts and building techniques are traditional Babylonian ones, utilising mudbricks and glazed tiles. The Bit Res complex, measuring no less than 217 x 167 m, seems to have had a pre-Hellenistic phase, but the main part was built under the Seleucids.[2] The temple

---

2   Kose and Bartel 1998, 93–196.

Fig. 21 | *Reconstruction of the Bit Res temple, Uruk.*

was inaugurated in 244 BC to the divine couple Anu-Antu, and it was the governor of Uruk, Anu-uballit, who undertook the construction. Antiochus II gave him the Greek name Nicharchus, as attested on a clay cylinder (YOS 1 52[3]), which records that the king gave the name Nicharchus to Anu-uballit who built the temple for the sake of the lives of Antiochus (II) and Seleucus (II), the kings.[4] Anu-uballit Nicharchus probably received his Greek name in connection with his appointment as governor.

The archives found in the temples of Uruk (Bit Res and the Irigal) contained two types of records: (1) traditional ones on clay tablets with cunei-

---

3   Falkenstein 1941, 4–5.
4   For a translation of the whole inscription, see Sherwin-White and Kuhrt 1993, 150.

form texts and (2) a new type with texts written in Greek or Aramaic on parchment or papyrus and sealed with bullae. Lindström's study (2003) of the seal impressions from Uruk reveals a ratio between bullae and tablets of approximately 10:1 (640 bullae and 61 tablets). The seal types from Babylonia during the Hellenistic period are, in general, new. Instead of cylinder seals or Achaemenid types of seals, elliptical seals in metal (usually as rings) were now the standard form of seal. Although the seal type is new, the iconography of the seals from Uruk display various sources of inspiration. Thus a significant number are in the Greek style, among them official seals showing royal portraits, royal symbols or Greek gods and heroes. Among the private seals, impressions of traditional Mesopotamian pictorial motifs dominate, with elements such as winged bulls and mythical animals, but they also include Greek motifs. A third group that emerged in the Hellenistic period displays, for instance, motifs from the zodiac; these probably refer to the city's fame as a centre of astronomy and astrology.

The strong continuation of traditional ways of life in Uruk is also attested by the known burial practices. Both Seleucid and Parthian burials have been found inside the city walls, and demonstrate continuation of the old tradition of burials being placed under houses. In Greek culture, this would have been unthinkable. Also, the few grave gifts, including pottery, show strong links to older Babylonian traditions. One of the few innovations is that the body, which used to be placed in a contracted position, was now laid out on its back.[5]

A very different picture is presented by two grave tumuli located at Frehat en-Nufegi, which is situated north of Uruk.[6] In the burial chamber of the western tumulus, four urns in traditional Babylonian style were found. Otherwise, the finds clearly reflect some of the most characteristic traits of Greek culture, including a golden wreath of olive leaves, which was probably originally placed on the urn of a male interment. Four strigils, items associated with the Greek gymnasium tradition, were also found close to this urn. The eastern tumulus shows an even stronger Greek tradition; the body was laid out on a *kline* with a golden wreath around the head, suggesting a symbolic presentation of the Greek symposium. Among the grave gifts is a wine amphora, possibly of eastern Mediterranean origin. The question of the identities of the individuals buried in the two tumuli arises. Were they Greek, of Greek descent or were they members of the local elite with Greek names or double names like Anu-uballit Nicharchus

5   Boehmer, Pedde, Salje 1995, 152-161.
6   Boehmer, Pedde, Salje 1995, 141–52.

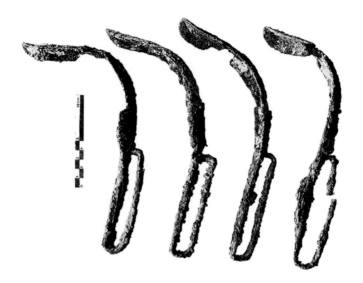

Fig. 22 | *Strigils from the western tumulus at Frehat en-Nufegi.*

or Anu-uballit Kephalon?[7] In addition to the grave gifts in the chambers already noted, the assemblage also includes typical local jars. As we shall see, however, this offers no indication of the ethnicity of the dead.

Babylon

At Babylon, a number of excavations (by British, French, German and Iraqi teams) have concentrated mainly on the earlier phases of the city, in particular the Neo-Babylonian. However, the most extensive project, the German excavations conducted under R. Koldewey (1914), focused on the later periods (i.e. from the Hellenistic to the Islamic period; Wetzel et al. 1957).

The Achaemenid/Neo-Babylonian palace, where Alexander stayed during his two visits to the city, was also where Seleucus resided before his new royal city of Seleucia-on-the-Tigris was built. We hear (Strabo XVI.1.5) that the *basileion* was moved.

Apart from fortifications and palaces, temples were the most monumental constructions. All the temples excavated to date in Babylonia were built in the traditional Mesopotamian tradition. Following Alexander's conquest, the Entemenanki ziggurat (with which the Esagila, the temple of Marduk, is associated) sat in a state of disrepair, and both Strabo (XVI.I.5) and Arrian (III.16.4, VII.17.1–4), together with the cuneiform tablet BCHP

---

7   See Doty 1988.

6, record that work to restore it was begun under Alexander. BCHP 6, *Ruin of Esagila Chronicle*[8], tells how Antiochus I fell on the ruins of the still unrepaired ziggurat, prayed in a Greek fashion, i.e. standing and with his arms lifted, and made an offering, before ordering the ruins to be removed. At some point, according to *Astronomical Diaries* 1 220–9 (BM 34093 + BM 35758 line 14), the debris of the Esagila was removed to the west bank of the Euphrates. However, despite its ruinous state, there seems to be no doubt that the Esagila was still in use during the Seleucid period (see also chapter 7).

The Homera mounds of Babylon consist of reused building material that was probably moved there from the Esagila area. Bricks with the stamp of Nebuchadnezzar II as well as a cylinder seal with his name were found among this material, and an important Greek monument, a theatre, was located on the middle of the mounds.[9]

The theatre had two building phases, of which the earliest, without a proskenion, probably dates from the time of Alexander or Seleucus. It may have been planned, and construction begun, during Alexander's lifetime, particularly considering that there must have been many Macedonians and Greeks in the city at this time and that a theatre could be used as a meeting place. The second phase may be related to Antiochus IV and his refounding of the city. A palaestra was attached to the theatre in a later period,[10] though it seems unlikely that the city would not have had a palaestra already during the time of Alexander.

The central area of the city to the east of the processional street, known as the Merkes, was a habitation area. Here, the old Neo-Babylonian houses seem to have continued more or less unchanged throughout the Hellenistic period, although a single house was rebuilt with a peristyle courtyard in the Greek style.[11] The area also included a large number of graves, including a number from the Seleucid period, some of which contained Greek-style terracottas and pottery.[12]

Seleucia

The little we know of the layout and architecture of Seleucia has already been presented in chapter 8. To date, no temple has been identified,

---

8   Finkel, van der Spek and Pirngruber, https://www.livius.org/sources/content/mesopotamian-chronicles-content/bchp-6-ruin-of-esagila-chronicle/
9   Mallwitz 1957.
10 Mallwitz 1957.
11 Reuther 1968, 80–92.
12 Reuther 1968, Taf. 94, 93.

although a small building next to the theatre may have been a temple in the Mesopotamian style, but probably dates from a later period. However, it is difficult to imagine that this royal city would ever have been without one or more large temples in the Greek style.

Terracottas from the Babylonian cities

Technically, Greek and Babylonian terracottas were very different traditions. Greek terracottas were traditionally made in a double mould with a vent hole on the back to let out gases during the firing phase. Very often they were covered with a thick lime wash onto which paint was added. In contrast, Mesopotamian terracottas were traditionally produced from a single (front) mould and with a flat back. In Babylonia during Seleucid and Parthian times, both methods can be found, together with a smaller number of handmade terracottas. The colours used for decoration are often red or pink, applied directly on the clay; sometimes the Greek tradition of applying a lime wash to the clay before painting is observed. The other principal colours used are blue, green and yellow. A few terracottas are glazed, as is the characteristic pottery (see below).

Large numbers of terracottas have been excavated from the city of Babylon; no less than 8,000 were found during the course of Koldewey's excavations.[13] There are significant numbers of unprovenanced examples in the British Museum and some in the Louvre. The Iraqi State Organization for Heritage and Antiquities began a large-scale excavation of Babylon in the late 1970s, but this was halted due to the Iran-Iraq War and then the First Gulf War. Consequently, Karvonen-Kannas (1995) published about 700 terracottas, of which more than the half are from the Iraqi Museum. Many of them derive from the so-called Eastern Hill, which was a residential area during the Hellenistic period.[14] Among the most popular types are standing naked women often holding their breasts with one or both hands, standing dressed women in oriental or Greek dress and reclining women, nude or dressed. The reclining male is a popular motif in Greek culture, whereas in Hellenistic Mesopotamia women are depicted in this pose. This type has been found in temples, graves and residential areas. The assemblage of male figurines includes quite a number of riders, among which the so-called Persian rider (see below) is quite common. At least one figurine of a standing man wearing a kausia, the typical Macedonian cap, has been

---

13 Koldewey 1914.
14 Note that Karvonen-Kannas 1995 uses the term 'Hellenistic' for both the Seleeucid and Parthian periods. It is, of course, often difficult to date terracottas any more precisely.

found. Mythological subjects, such as Herakles, standing or seated, Eros, Eros and Psyche, and Aphrodite, were popular. Although most of the terracottas are of low quality, a few are very fine, such as that of a standing woman in chiton and cloak with a melon coiffure, suggesting a date in the late fourth or third century,[15] made in a double mould and with a vent hole on the back. Another high-quality example is of Europa on the bull, also with a vent hole on the back.[16]

The terracotta assemblage from the American excavations in Seleucia includes about 3,000 figurines from the Seleucid and Parthian periods. These came particularly from two areas, of which one (Block B) seems to have been a residential area; the other area, Trial Trench 4, seems, at least in the Parthian period, to have been a temple precinct.[17] Like the Babylon examples, those from Seleucia include both traditional oriental and Greek types. As at Babylon, the Seleucid and Parthian types are often related; there seem to be only a few new types, with most examples displaying a continuation of Seleucid styles and types. It is not surprising that, compared to Babylon, the 'Greek' element is stronger and, technically, Greek techniques dominate. Thus the use of double mould and vent holes is common, as is the use of lime wash on the surface of the clay – a tradition not previously known in the Near East.[18] The quality of the figurines from the American excavations is not impressive; they were a rather quickly made mass production.

More than 9,000 terracottas have been recorded from the Italian excavations. They were found in all the areas investigated and, again, the Seleucid and Parthian figurines are often similar and there were only fairly few new types added in Parthian times. The assemblage is characterised by many Greek motifs, such as Greek gods, theatrical masks and athletes, and extensive use of the double mould; this was also used for traditional local motifs. An unusually large number of the terracottas (3,000) were found in a small sounding on the southern side of the north agora. Undoubtedly these are remains from a large terracotta workshop that was active here. An impressive publication, including all the terracottas from the Italian excavations and most of those from the American (Menegazzi 2014), offers a very good impression of the richness of Seleucid and Parthian figurines from the capital of Babylonia. Less than 10% were found in Seleucid layers,

---

15   Karvonen-Kannas 1995 no. 85.
16   Karvonen-Kannas 1995, no. 274.
17   van Ingen 1939.
18   See Menegazzi 2014, 8 table 2 for a comparison of the techniques used in Seleucia, Babylon, Uruk and Susa.

Fig. 23 | *Terracotta of a standing woman in Greek dress found in Seleucia on the Tigris. H. 36,9 cm. Unusual technique with hands and the missing head of marble attached with stucco. Remains of red and blue colour on the dress.*

but this is due to the simple reason that these levels have been reached in only a few places (see chapter 8).

The published Seleucid and Parthian terracotta figurines from Uruk were found mainly in the area of the Bit Res sanctuary and the Irigal, and not in situ.[19] They display a mix of old motifs, such as the standing naked female figurine, and Greek motifs, including gods such as Heracles, Aphrodite and Eros. The quality of the published figurines is generally crude.

The terracottas from the three Babylonian cities show varying degrees of continuity and change; there is a continuation of the Neo-Babylonian terracotta tradition in terms of types, styles and techniques versus the intro-

---

19   Ziegler 1962.

Fig. 24 | *Terracottas from Babylon. Two nude females (H. 19.91 and 38.14 cm) – in Babylonian style and Greek technique.*

duction of Greek motifs and techniques. A significant number could be described as hybrid or cross-cultural, combining, for instance, a Babylonian motif with a Greek technique or vice versa.[20] A particular difficulty in analysing this material is that we are dealing not only with Seleucid but also Parthian terracottas, without being able to follow a chronological development from one period to the next.[21]

---

20 Langin-Hooper 2007 is a very thorough analysis of the Babylonian terracotta figurines from Hellenistic Babylonia with a focus on social identities. Undoubtedly, this is an interesting approach to the terracottas, but this group of material can only ever offer a small part of the larger picture.
21 Karvonen-Kannas 1995.

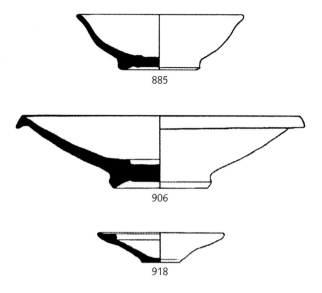

885

906

918

Pottery from the Babylonian cities

The most common type of fine ware in Babylonia during the Seleucid period is an alkaline glazed ware in green, white or yellow. Greek shapes, like the fish plate, the bowl with angular profile and outturned rim, and the echinus bowl, were popular forms, together with a number of traditional shapes, particularly of bowls and a type of amphora with two loop handles on the shoulders instead of the vertical handles from neck to shoulder used in Greece. A contemporary type of fine ware, the so-called eggshell ware, on the other hand, was produced in the traditional shapes, with just a few exceptions. Coarse wares, such as cooking ware, also include typical Greek shapes.[22]

Unfortunately, the pottery from the Italian excavations of Seleucia-on-the-Tigris has not been published in full (although some short articles have appeared).[23] The large amount of pottery recovered during the course of the excavations in Seleucia shows that here too there was a mix of Greek shapes and locally made glazed ware and common ware, as at the other Babylonian sites, though perhaps with a larger proportion of Greek shapes. Not surprisingly, it seems that more Greek shapes were made locally at

---

22 See Hannestad 1983.

23 See https://www.centroscavitorino.it/index.php/en/projects/iraq-eng/iraq-seleucia-on-the-tigris
    See also Hannestad 1983, 97–105 for Hellenistic pottery from southern Mesopotamia.

Seleucia than in the old cities. Thus, not only Greek black-glazed shapes, but also lagynoi, West Slope ware and Megarian bowls are found in the glazed-ware assemblage of Seleucia. Imported Greek pottery is fairly rare; but in the Parthian period, imported eastern sigillata A ware was quite common.[24]

Hellenistic pottery from Uruk has been published by Strommenger (1967) and discussed in detail by Hannestad (1983, 102). The finds derive mainly from the two sancturaries Res and Irigal. It is closely related to pottery from Seleucia, but with fewer Greek shapes and very few Greek imports.

Stamp impressions from the Babylonian cities

The more than 25,000 clay seal impressions found in the archive building in Seleucia[25] show a high proportion of Greek styles and motifs, including gods such as Zeus, Athena, Artemis (often blended with the old Sumerian goddess Nanaia), Apollo, Eros, Tyche and several others. Some show portraits (male, female and children) with several identified as royal portraits. Thus one has been identified as Seleucus;[26] others display Seleucus' anchor (see fig. 11). These royal seal impressions were made by official seals, the majority of which carried only inscriptions (such as *halikes* and Seleucia, i.e. salt tax paid at Seleucia) and the year according to the Seleucid era. These seal impressions were found in large numbers in the archive. They clearly present the dealings of the central administration, which probably explains the strong Greek influence.

Conclusion

In general terms, these three groups of artefacts together clearly reflect the hybrid nature of the culture of the Babylonian cities. The terracottas were very often hybrid in terms of technique, and their find spots within the three cities demonstrate that both locals and Greeks used the same terracottas. A similar picture can be seen with regard to pottery. The local production technique is also used for Greek shapes, and local and Greek shapes are used together. Seleucia has revealed the broadest repertoire of Greek shapes in the local glazed ware. The seal impressions show definite differences. Thus, in Seleucia large numbers are clearly Greek, displaying Greek inscriptions, portraits in the Greek style and a large variety of Greek

---

24 A number of imported Greek sherds derive already from Archaic-period Babylon, with a growing number dated to the fourth century BC (Deubner 1957, 51–8).

25 Invernizzi 2004.

26 Invernizzi 2004 vol. 1, Se 1.

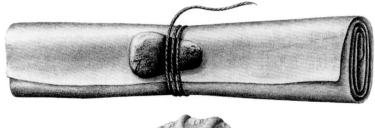

Fig. 26 | *Attachment of bullae to the documents. Uruk.*

Fig. 27 | *Official seal impression from Seleucia-on-the-Tigris. One of several seal impressions with a similar inscription: alikes; Seleukeias, HP, epitelon.*

Fig. 28 | *One of the finest portrait seal impressions found in Seleucia.*

gods. In Uruk, on the other hand, where the seal impressions/terracottas were found mainly in the temples, we see both old local motifs and a number of Greek gods; the quality is generally lower.

Susiana and the Persian Gulf

Susa

Architectural remains of the third century are not easy to detect at Susa,[27] but it seems that no area of the site was more densely inhabited than in earlier times. The propylon of the Achaemenid palace was apparently outside the city in this period, since a Greek burial urn has been found here.[28] The so-called Ville Royale saw some changes during the Seleucid period (level VII), which may indicate the adoption of an orthogonal street grid. One house with a large peristyle court has been identified; it was decorated in the Greek style too, with mural paintings, and provided with a tiled roof.

Terracottas from the Seleucid and Parthian periods are frequent finds in Susa.[29] As in Babylonia, they show a wide variety of Greek and Oriental types, and are generally of high quality. About 60% are mould-made, either in a single mould or a double mould. Among the Greek heroes and gods, Heracles, Eros and Aphrodite are common. Musicians also appear frequently, as do female figurines in the Greek style. Among the handmade figurines, the figure of the so-called Persian rider is particularly popular.

The pottery assemblage includes some imported black-glazed sherds,[30] but is otherwise closely related to that from Babylonia. It comprises, for example, the typical glazed ware, including a mix of Greek and local shapes, and also eggshell ware.[31]

Failaka

On the small island of Failaka in the Persian Gulf, known as Icarus to the Greeks, Danish (and later French) excavations have revealed a small Greek-style temple with two columns in antis.[32] The columns are Ionian but with bases in the Persian style. Typical Greek traits include the cult statue, of which only parts of the base remain, that was erected in the cella

---

27   Martinez-Sève 2010.
28   Martinez-Sève 2002b, 39.
29   Martinez-Sève 2002a; 2004.
30   Clairmont 1956-1957.
31   See Bourcharlat 1993.
32   Jeppesen 1989.

Fig. 29 | *The Hellenis-*
tic temple on Failaka.

and the altar in front of the entrance to the temple. The temple was surrounded by a defensive wall, which was later strengthened with a moat
and a new gate. A stele with a long Greek inscription – a message from a
Seleucid king – was placed in front of an ante of the temple. Unfortunately,
the dating of the inscription is unreadable, but it is undoubtedly later than
the time of Seleucus.[33]

Nonetheless, Seleucid soldiers must have come to the island in the
first decades of the third century, possibly for short periods only. This is
confirmed by finds at a small sanctuary at Tell Khazneh, where the coin

33 See Jeppesen 1960; Rouché and Sherwin-White 1985; Jeppesen 1989; Hannestad 2019.

hoard mentioned in chapter 6 was found.[34] The latest coin in the hoard is one of Seleucus I, and the hoard was probably buried around 285 or earlier. Together with stray bronze coins dating from the time of Alexander and to the later years of Seleucus found on the site, the hoard was probably left here during one or more visits by a group of soldiers. The island of this period is described by Arrian (VII.19) with reference to information from Aristoboulus.

Outside the fortress was a building which seems to have been a terracotta workshop, since quite a number of moulds and figurines were recovered from it.[35] We find the familiar mix of traditional Mesopotamian figurines and new Greek-style terracottas. The so-called Persian rider figurines suggest strong ties to Susiana. The unusual figurines of the so-called Parthian kings,[36] from the late phase of the fortress, suggest continued connections northwards to Spasinou Charax; this is also attested by four coins.[37] Connelly suggests that a few figurines were imported from Asia Minor or the Levant. Despite the location of the island and the fact that most of the coins found here are Arabian imitations of Alexander coins, there is no evidence of figurines connected with the Arabian mainland, such as the figurines found at Thaj.[38]

The rich collection of pottery from the fortress and sanctuary[39] clearly indicates strong ties with Mesopotamia and Susiana.[40] The typical fine wares of these areas, glazed ware and eggshell ware, are richly presented on Failaka. In contrast, examples of pottery connected with the Arabian mainland are few (the so-called Arabian red- and black-washed ware, coarse red ware, etc[41]; called Arabian ware by French archaeologists[42]). Characteristic of Hannestad's period II[43] are a few very characteristic bowls closely related to Nabataean ware.[44]

---

34 Amandry and Callot 1988; Houghton and Lorber 2002, 107.
35 Mathiesen 1982; Connelly 1990.
36 Mathiesen 1982, nos 67, 68.
37 For thorough discussions of the terracottas and their origins, see Mathiesen 1982, 72; Connelly 1990, 209–20.
38 That Thaj was a centre for pottery production is indicated by large dumps found outside the city wall. Franke and Gierlichs 2011, 170 Abb. 2.
39 Hannestad 1983; Courbet 1984; Bernard, Gachet and Salles 1990.
40 For a discussion of this, see in particular Hannestad 1983, 79.
41 Hannestad 1983, 49-50, 69.
42 Bernard, Gachet and Salles 1990, 262–5.
43 See Hannestad 1983, 78–9.
44 See Hannestad 1983, 51–2.

Bactria

Ai Khanoum

The dating of Ai Khanoum, in particular its early phase/phases, has been much discussed in recent years (see also chapter 8). The historical sources (Plut. *Vit.Alex.*[45]; Appian *Syr* 57; see also chapter 8), with their stress on Alexander and Seleucus as important city founders, suggest that it was founded under one of them. Both campaigned in Bactria and we know that Alexander founded a number of Alexandrias – of which Ai Khanoum could, in principle, be one. However, studies of the coins and perhaps also of the pottery may suggest that only the ramparts (or parts of them), the heroon of Kineas and the first phase of the main temple belong to such an early period.[46] Furthermore, the layout of the long main street, so typical of Seleucid cities, probably belongs to the first phase. The current consensus is that Antiochus I, either as co-regent or when king himself, holds the main responsibility for the initiation of Ai Khanoum. The city as it could be seen when the French excavations stopped, following the Russian invasion of Afghanistan in 1979, is a later phase from the time after Seleucid rule. Some scholars suppose that in this period the city was called Eucratidaea (Strabo XI.11[47]). It was abandoned in about 145 BC, probably due to attacks by nomads.

The name Kineas may refer to a general of Alexander or Seleucus, who was given the task to supervise the city in its initial phase.[48] The structure underwent four building phases. In its initial phase, the heroon was a rather small building constructed of mudbricks – the standard building material for most of the city throughout its lifetime. A krepis of three steps surrounded a temple that has a pronaos wider than its cella and two columns in antis columns (stone bases and probably wooden columns). It was probably built during the reign of Antiochos.[49] In this phase the building bears a resemblance to Greek heroa in terms of layout with a pronaos wider than the cella, such as the heroon of Kalydon[50] or Macedonian tombs

---

45 https://www.livius.org/articles/misc/alexander-s-city-foundations/?
46 See Martinez-Sève 2014.
47 See Martinez-Sève 2014, 267.
48 Bernard 1973.
49 The famous Clearchos inscription found in the sanctuary states that it was set up in the temenos of Kineas. The inscription with the Delphic maximes has been dated by Rougemont to the first half of the third century (2012, 202, 204-208).
50 Dyggve, Poulsen and Rhomaios 1934.

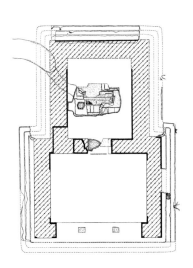

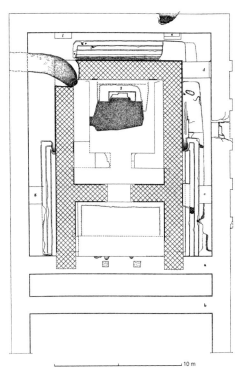

Fig. 30 | *Plan of the Heroon of Kineas. Left first phase, right second phase.*

like the tomb of Lefkadia.[51] Kineas' sarcophagus – we may assume – was interred below the structure in a pit of unbaked bricks that predates the heroon itself. A circular hole in the lid of the sarcophagus was intended for libations that could be poured through the floor above. The pottery found in the heroon of Kineas appears to be contemporary with that from the main sanctuary suggesting a contemporary date. The layout of the heroon is changed in its second phase, larger and more like a Greek temple in antis; instead of the krepis it stood on a podium.

The first phase of this temple (known as the Temple with Indented Niches) has been dated by a bronze coin in the filling of the temple terrace,[52] which suggests that also the heroon was built at this time. The temple is very different from a standard Greek temple.[53] It was a square building standing on a platform, which in the initial phases was surrounded by three steps, reminiscent of the Greek krepis. The walls and krepis were whitewashed. On the outer walls are the stepped niches that have given

---

51   Lerner is sceptical about the comparison with Macedonian tombs (2004, 384-385); he does not consider the heroon of Kalydon.

52   Martinez-Sève 2014, 32.

53   Mairs 2013.

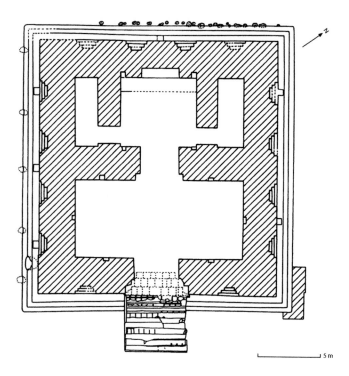

Fig. 31 | *Plan of the Temple with Indented Niches, Ai Khanoum.*

the temple its name. Inside there is a pronaos and, in the very first phase (phase V), a cella; in the next phase (IV) this was altered to a smaller cella that was flanked by two corridors connected to it. The shape of the building is square and it had a flat roof. The building material is mudbrick strengthened with a wooden framework, as for most of the buildings of the city. In the vestibule a number of over life-sized terracotta statues were found. In the cella was a marble foot from an acrolithic statue; it was clad in a sandal decorated with a thunderbolt, and therefore the main deity of the temple was probably Zeus, possibly sometimes identified with a local god or Bel. An interesting find was made, not in situ, in the southern corridor: a medallion in gilded silver showing Cybele drawn in a chariot by two lions and Nike as charioteer coming to an oriental sanctuary. Whereas most of the relief is in the Greek style, the sanctuary and the god or priest standing on top of it are in traditional Oriental style, which could also be found in Mesopotamia. This find and others probably belong to the last phase, before the city was overwhelmed by nomads (see Francfort 1984 for the finds inside the temple). The temenos may have been shared by more gods, since a number of pedestals and two smaller temples, more in the Greek style, with two columns in antis, were found here (see Mairs 2013 for a discussion of the non-Greek style of the temple).

Fig. 32 | *Gilded silver plate found in the Temple with indented niches, Ai Khanoum. D. 25 cm. The motif shows the goddess Cybele and Nike standing on a chariot drawn by lions. To the right a priest on a high-stepped altar in Oriental style.*

A temple located outside the walls has a very similar plan,[54] though here we are clearly dealing with three cellae. An older and smaller temple of similar plan was apparently found below this temple.

The large palace excavated at Ai Khanoum was probably the residence of the satrap, while part of the complex contained the treasury. What we know of the palace dates to a late phase of the city, probably to the time of the Greco-Bactrian kings. A large courtyard (136.80 x 108.10 m) surrounded by Corinthian columns (altogether 116 columns) forms the centre of the complex and is surrounded by a structure, or rather a number of buildings, with various functions. Altogether the complex is more closely related to Greek architecture than Achaemenid. A typical eastern trait is the use of many interior corridors; this is also seen on a smaller scale in the governor's palace at Jebel Khalid, and thus dates back to the time of Seleucus or Antiochus. A columnar vestibule or hall on the southern side leads to what must have been rooms for private functions. Among the rooms on the western side is a treasury, in which rich finds were made despite the looting of the city around 145 BC. Jars left in the treasury were identified by inscriptions in ink or graffiti; mainly in Greek, a few in Aramaic.

---

54 Bernard 1976, 304, fig. 11.

Fig. 33 | *Ai Khanoum today after war and looting with heavy machines.*

At present, no house finds from the earliest period of the city have been published. They must, of course, have existed, but the excavators concentrated on the well-preserved houses of the upper layers. The large houses excavated in the southern part of the city and the villa outside the walls apparently all belong to the period of the Greco-Bactrian kings.[55] The houses excavated near the heroon of Kineas and the main temple are much more modest, and also belong to the second century BC. A typical element of the houses is a hall with two columns in antis opening to a courtyard.

The gymnasium also derives from the period of the Greco-Bactrian kings.[56] Remains from the earliest phase of building (phase VI) suggest that houses initially covered at least part of the area; it is not known if the early gymnasium was located here or at another site within the walls. Most prob-

---

55 Lecuyot 2013.
56 Veuve 1987.

ably, it was in this area but on a much smaller scale than its later manifestation. Considering the importance of this institution in the Hellenistic period, it is unthinkable that the city would have been without a gymnasium in the Seleucid period.

Turning to the burial customs of Ai Khanoum, it is clear that they demonstrate a strong Greek tradition, with burials located outside the walls. Excavations of a mausoleum revealed that it had been used through several generations. Inscriptions on three of the jars in which bones were collected for reburial are in Greek, as are two fragmentary inscriptions found in connection with the mausoleum. The entrance to the tomb was blocked by a fragmentary tombstone decorated with a relief showing a young man in a long cloak, but otherwise naked, in the Greek tradition, and with a petasos hanging from his shoulder. However, his long hair is a distinctly non-Greek trait.[57]

The pottery assemblage from Ai Khanoum also provides evidence of Greek influence. In particular, a fine grey-black pottery not only imitates Greek shapes but also the linked palmettes on bowls and plates[58] that are characteristic of Athens in the early third century;[59] this was the period when the so-called black-slipped pottery (or often red-slipped) began to be produced in Ai Khanoum. Before the introduction of the latter, a traditional whitish pottery continued in Achaemenid shapes but had already adopted Greek shapes too. Evidence of continuous Greek influence through to the time when the city was part of the kingdom of the Greco-Bactrian kings is evidenced by imitations of the so-called Megarian bowls, the production of which began in Athens in 225.[60]

The lowering of the dating of many of the buildings in Ai Khanoum partly depends on the dating of these moulded bowls, which are undoubtedly imitations of the Athenian Megarian bowls. This was a much more popular shape in Ai Khanoum than in Mesopotamia and Susiana. Imitations of the so-called Pergamene relief ware also appeared.[61] Interestingly, the glazed ware so popular in Mesopotamia and Susiana is not found in central Asia. The closeness in many ways to Greek architecture, pottery, etc. in this late period is often connected with the anabasis of Antiochos III and a new influx of Greek soldiers under the Greco-Bactrian kings. Greek is the most common language used for inscriptions found in the city –

57 Bernard 1972; Hannestad 2013, 110.
58 Lyonnet 2012, figs 8, 10; Lecyout 2013, fig. 107:7–8.
59 Rotroff 1997, 143.
60 Rotroff 1982.
61 Hübner 1993.

whether on stone, clay, parchment or papyrus.[62] Among the names found in the inscriptions, Greek ones are by far the most common, with just a few Iranian examples. Inscriptions on jars found in the treasury confirm continued contact with the Mediterranean world, since the shapes of the letters are very similar to those used in Egypt in the second century BC.

Jebel Khalid

The settlement of Jebel Khalid on the western bank of the Euphrates (see chapter 8) reveals a different pattern of material culture. The so-called governor's palace, situated on the highest point of the jebel and protected by an inner wall, is well preserved and dates from the third century.[63] From here, there was a fine view both up and down the river and its valley. As in the Macedonian homeland, the palace was centred around a peristyle court with Doric columns, flanked on the northern and southern sides by what must have been official rooms for audiences and banquets. The large northern room had one column, its floor was covered with marble slabs and the walls were decorated with paintings in the so-called Pompeian First Style. The only element that clearly differs significantly from Greek and Macedonian palaces and villas is the corridors with narrow doorways that led between the courtyard and the entrances to the official rooms. These corridors are very common in the Near East (e.g. Anu-Antum Temple at Uruk and the governor's palace in Ai Khanoum). In the long corridor on the western side on the lowest floor level, two official Seleucid seal impressions and a coin of Seleucus II were found. Related to this structure is the so-called Citadel Palace at Dura Europos. Part of the second phase of the palace, probably dating from the second century, is preserved; here too, a peristyle courtyard seems to be the centre of the palace and on the preserved southern side are official rooms very similar to those of Jebel Khalid, though without the corridors leading towards the courtyard.

One temple has been excavated at Jebel Khalid.[64] It was built of limestone and in what one might call a simplified Doric style with faceted, not fluted, columns, triglyphs and metopes, but apparently without taenia and guttae. The layout is hexastyle amphiprostyle with a broad cella which had a tripartite adyton. The temple measures 17 x 13 m on the exterior. In the temenos, marble toes from two different statues have been found; these were clearly imported to the site.[65] The beginning of the temple building

---

62 Rapin 1983; Bernard 2008.
63 Clarke 2002, 47–8; 2003.
64 Clarke 2006.
65 See Clarke 2009 for the marbles from Jebel Khalid.

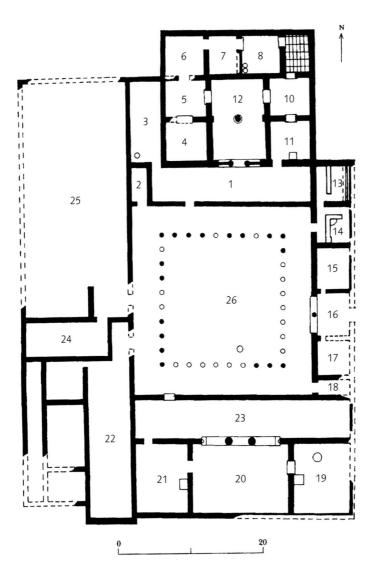

Fig. 34 | *Plan of the palace at Jebel Khalid.*

dates to the first half of the third century, based on pottery and coins from a deposit.[66] Compared to the elegant governor's palace, the temple represents what one might call a provincial or perhaps an amateurish version of a Doric temple.

How did the individual houses of the long blocks of houses that characterise many of the cities of the Seleucid colonies function? The housing insula excavated at Jebel Khalid is one extremely well-excavated example[67]

66 Clarke 2006.
67 Jackson 2014.

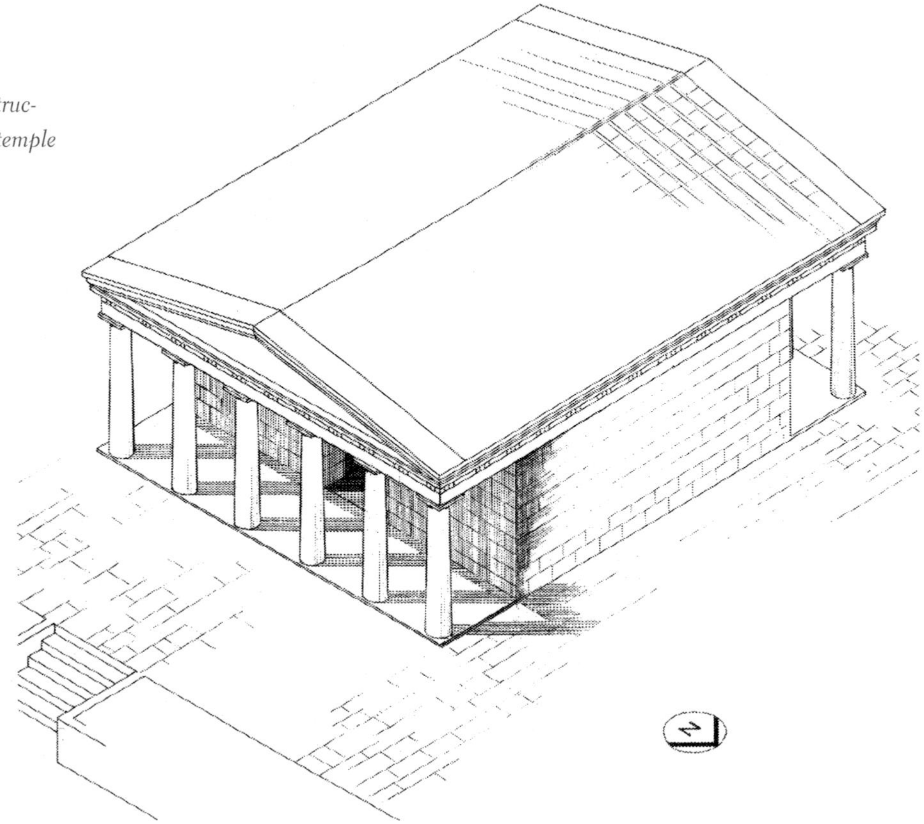

Fig. 35 | *Reconstruction of the Doric temple at Jebel Khalid.*

that might help us to answer such questions. Here there were two main phases (A and B), and from their very beginning the houses were of various sizes, although all were fairly large. They were built of rubble and mud-bricks directly on the bedrock, and at least some of the houses had pitched roofs, based on the number of tiles found. One house, the House of the Painted Frieze, is no less than 772 m². In the earliest phase (A), one of the rooms of this most important house had walls that were probably painted a deep red; in phase B they were painted in masonry style with a figured frieze. The room was probably used for receptions and perhaps ritual functions. Other than this space in the largest house, the rooms of this and the other houses generally seem to have had a practical character. Two coins of Antiochus I are noted as having been found on the bedrock below the primary floor level,[68] and thus Jackson suggests that this insula was built in the middle of the third century (2014, 8). However, it may of course have been built during the lifetime of Antiochus. The insula was abandoned

---

68 Jackson 2014, 8, fig. 1.11.

(only the buildings and waste were left behind) in the late 70s or early 60s BC, still in Seleucid times.

Terracottas have been recovered from all the excavated areas. The majority were made on the site and are rather crude and without traces of paint or white slip. Technically, most were made in a double mould, but they are modelled on the front only. Vent holes also suggest influence from the west. The most common types are females (often only the head is preserved) and the so-called Persian rider – which is often handmade.[69] A few specimens can be identified or tentatively identified as gods: including Aphrodite, Astarte (normally a special type made from a single mould on a plaque), Dionysus, Eros and Attis.

The pottery from Jebel Khalid is, to a large extent, locally made and imitates shapes from the west, such as echinus bowls, fish plates and, for graves, unguentaria. Imports from the west, mainly from Antioch are also common, including black-glaze ware, eastern sigillata A ware and Megarian bowls. In contrast, pottery from the east (from Mesopotamia, on the other side of the river) is not common and consists mainly of green-glazed ware, but in Greek shapes.[70] Rhodian wine amphoras, which have rarely been found east of the Euphrates, were imported to Jebel Khalid, particularly in the second half of the third century and the first half of the second.

Thus this settlement, located as far east as the western bank of the Euphrates, clearly had its strongest ties with the west, particularly with Antioch-on-the-Orontes.

Conclusion

When looking at the material culture of daily life in the different regions of the Seleucid Empire, we see, to varying degrees, a mix of Greek and what we may call 'local' elements; the exception to this rule is the region of Seleucus' final conquest, western Asia Minor, where Greek culture had already existed for generations. The material culture of Early Hellenistic Syria, which had also been familiar with Greek culture for centuries (and vice versa) but had not housed a large Greek population, reveals a strong Greek cultural influence; this is probably due to immigrants from Greece making up a large proportion of the population at this time.

Further east, in Babylonia, Mesopotamia, Persia and Bactria, we find surprising combinations of local and Greek elements. There is not a single

---

69 See Jackson 2006, pl. VIII for the frequency of the types found in the housing insula.
70 Jackson and Tidmarsh 2011, 431–96; Jackson in Clarke 2002, 101–24; Jackson 2014, 580–1.

Fig. 36 | *Ostrakon from Babylon. The inscription is in Greek and probably from the early third century BC, including the Greek name Ballaros, which was common in the Greek cities in Asia Minor. The ostrakon probably attests a payment to a Greek soldier from the garrison of the city (see Sherwin-White, S. 1982).*

uniform material culture that characterises this large area. Babylonia and Susiana display some similar traits which, to a large extent, can also be detected in the material culture of Parthian times, just as the royal city of Seleucia-on-the-Tigris, with its large Greek population, continued to enact Greek customs, such as utilising a theatre, during the Parthian period. We have also seen that terrracottas from the Seleucid and the Parthian periods are very similar, with just a few new types being introduced. Nonetheless, the old cities of Mesopotamia in many ways maintained their original culture, religion and daily life. There were, however, new elements to experience, such as coins, the official language (see the ostracon with a Greek inscription from Babylon: Sherwin-White 1982) and, undoubtedly, a number of issues related to bureaucracy, such as the new seal types and types of seal impressions. But, if we look closely at two important though normally modest elements of material culture – terracottas and pottery – we find an interesting mix of old and new, and, indeed, that both local and Greek versions were used by both the indigenous and Greek populations. In contrast, the old temples of Babylon were restored in the traditional style; typically, religion is less, and more slowly, affected by new ideas. Even Ai Khanoum, a new foundation, presents the example of its main temple being, in all phases, constructed in a completely non-Greek style. This is particularly surprising given the existence of the gymnasium and, not least, the palace, with its exquisite stone columns from the last phase of the city's existence. Furthermore, items of everyday use, such as pottery, quickly adopted the new Greek shapes and, in post-Seleucid phases, utilised the most up-to-date Greek shapes.

Thus, in many respects, the material culture of the Seleucid Empire displays a noted regionalism. Within one region there may also have been variations, and the new and, particularly, the large cities unsurprisingly reveal a stronger Greek emphasis than the old cities.

CHAPTER 10

Conclusion

When Seleucus died in 281 BC, the Diadoch period came to an end. Forty years of conflict between Alexander's ambitious generals, who around 15–20 years after his death had each assumed the royal title themselves, had totally altered his empire and split it into four kingdoms, the largest of which was Seleucus'. However, the expansion of his realm was not based on a plan, except perhaps for his eastern anabasis, which resulted from the weakening of the Upper Satrapies after the war between Antigonus and Eumenes, when several of the satraps appointed in Babylon were killed or replaced by newly appointed men. Rather, Seleucus' empire was built up gradually in the period following the Babylonian War against Antigonus, essentially in three phases: (1) the campaign in the east in which he conquered a number of the Upper Satrapies after many of them had been left without their Macedonian satraps, and made an agreement with the Indian king Sandrocottus; (2) the battle at Ipsus 301 did not lead to him acquiring much new territory, apart from northern Syria, but it did result in his empire becoming part of the Mediterranean world; (3) following the battle against Lysimachus, he acquired Asia Minor north of the Taurus.

Before he set out for his return to Macedonia, Seleucus took the precaution of appointing his son Antiochus (I Soter) 'King of Asia'; he probably had in mind events following Alexander's death, when no successor had been appointed. Long before, he had trained his son as a general, as we know from the record of the battle at Ipsus (chapter 4), and, since 294, Antiochus had been his co-regent. Thus he had taken care to ensure that his son was already an experienced leader and ruler.

Seleucus bequeathed his son a military monarchy in which the king, his friends and the army ruled supreme. There is no evidence that Seleucus attempted to make his empire a homogeneous unit; instead, the different geographical units to a large extent maintained their own cultures. Just a few Greek elements were introduced across the whole empire. Thus Greek became the official language and Greek-style coined monetisation encompassed the whole realm.

Central to Seleucus maintaining his hold across the empire was the generation of sufficient revenue. It was probably only through revenue-raising processes that most of the population of the empire came into contact with the king, and then only via his authorities. The level of taxation must have varied over time, depending on the needs of the king. War was expensive and demanded both men and money, but a standing army was required in times of peace as well. A further imposition that must have affected, sometimes strongly, the lives of local people was Seleucus' colonisation programme, which was continued by Antiochus. This brought large numbers of Macedonians and Greeks, soldiers and veterans, to settle in the conquered territories. Extensive land was required to meet the needs of these colonisers, not only to build new settlements but also for agricultural activities to support the colonists, their families and their slaves. It is not easy to estimate the extent to which this policy resulted in local people being moved from their farmsteads and villages. Nonetheless, in the region of Ai Khanoum it is clear that earlier settlements from the Achaemenid period were destroyed or simply abandoned when the city was built (see chapter 8).

Seleucus' army must, to a large extent, have included not only Macedonians and Greeks (of which many were mercenaries) but also men from those parts of the empire with strong warrior traditions. Alexander had been able to recruit soldiers from his homeland to replace men lost and those no longer able to fight, and, despite protests from his Macedonian soldiers, he also included Persians in his army. Ptolemy adopted a similar strategy, and apparently surprised Hieronymus/Diodorus Siculus by using trained Egyptians as combat soldiers (Diod. Sic. XIX.80.4).

The creation of an empire was not something that Seleucus planned from the moment he became satrap of Babylonia; rather, the opportunity to do so arose at the end of the Babylonian War. From this point onwards he opportunistically acquired more land whenever possible. His strength was, first and foremost, that he had the patience to wait until the chance of success was high. In this way, he stands in contrast to Antigonus, who, time and time again, lost his patience and did not calculate the risks inherent in his actions. This is evident from his eastern campaign against Eumenes, when, for instance, he chose a short and difficult route instead of the slower but easier Royal Road to travel from Susiana to Persia (see chapter 3), which led to a great loss of men; and, again, when he and Demetrius, with his fleet, moved against Ptolemy despite warnings of bad weather. Furthermore, during his last campaign against Lysimachus he chose a lowland route that was made impassable by rain; again he suffered substantial losses (see chapter 4).

In contrast, Appian characterises Seleucus as: 'Always lying in wait for the neighbouring nations, strong in arms and persuasive in council, he acquired [followed by a long list of territories]' (*Syr.* 11.55).[1] Seleucus apparently also had a talent for dealing with people, which in war meant that he was often able to persuade opposing soldiers to desert in order to join him and his army. He apparently did not like Lysimachus, and Seleucus and Antigonus seem never to have been on good terms. Among his satrapal and royal colleagues, Ptolemy and Peithon (until his death at Antigonus' hands) seem to have been his closest comrades in war. With Peithon he undoubtedly sanctioned the murder of Perdiccas and, later, they worked together as satraps of Media and Babylonia. Seleucus fled to Ptolemy after Antigonus had returned to Babylon following his campaign against Eumenes and having killed Peithon. He campaigned with Ptolemy, both as an admiral and a general, before returning to Babylon with the latter's assistance.

Arrian, himself a general, considered Seleucus 'the greatest king of those who succeeded Alexander, of the most royal mind, and ruling over the greatest extent of territory' (VII.22.5). Pausanias states that he is 'persuaded that Seleucus was the most righteous and in particular the most religious of the kings. Firstly, it was Seleucus who sent back to the Branchidae for the Milesians the bronze Apollo that had been carried by Xerxes to Ecbatana in Persia. Secondly, when he founded Seleucia on the river Tigris and brought to it Babylonian colonists, he spared the wall of Babylon as well as the sanctuary of Bel, near which he permitted the Chaldeans to live' (I.16). How Pausanias came to this conclusion is not known; we may assume he based his opinion on a now lost literary source or, less probably, that this was told to him by his guide at the Athenian Agora, when he studied the bronze statue of Seleucus there.

Seleucus would undoubtedly have seen himself as a warrior king, as defined much later in the Suda lexicon (Austin 1981, no. 37): 'Monarchical power (*basileia*) is given to men neither by nature nor by law; it is given to those who are capable of commanding troops and dealing prudently with [political] matters' (see also Chaniotis 2005, 57). As Chaniotis stresses, the Diadochs used the title 'king' unaccompanied by an ethnic name. Indeed, for Seleucus, with his ethnically mixed empire, this would not have been possible. However, he never forgot, and nor did he let others forget, his

---

1 'He was a realist, a pragmatist, a calculator. His will was very strong' – a description of a British field marshal of the Second World War (Alanbrooke) (Fraser 1991) could actually fit Seleucus.

Macedonian origin;[2] and he often stressed how special it was to have fought with Alexander. Furthermore, Seleucus' admiration of Alexander is clear in his adoption of Alexander's policy of following up conquest by settling colonisers in newly acquired territories.

Seleucus did not have a permanent capital, much like during the so-called *Reisekönigtum* ('itinerant kingship') of Medieval Germany (or, for that matter, England or Denmark) when the king did not stay in one city, but travelled around his realm, staying in a number of different locations known as royal cities. The enormous size of the Seleucid Empire, even before the ultimate victory at Corupedium, demanded that the king, his court and his army were regularly present in the various regions. Antiochus' appointment as co-regent over the east, after which he stayed mainly in Babylon, meant that Seleucus could concentrate on the newly conquered territory of northern Syria and his enormous colonisation programme there. Suspicion between father and son seems never to have been an issue.

Seleucus was not born into the uppermost Macedonian elite, and this initially limited his promotion. Whilst Braund, by stressing his youth, implies his age was the reason Seleucus did not receive a satrapy at Babylon (2003, 23), to my mind, it was due to the fact that he did not belong to the circle of life guards (*somatophylakes*) and his family probably did not have the same social status. This is confirmed by the marriage alliances of the period. Both Ptolemy and Lysimachus married daughters of Antipater after Alexander's death; Seleucus, however, continued to be married to his Persian wife. It was not until Demetrius had lost most of his wealth and army, and was in a very tricky situation, following the battle at Ipsus, that a marriage was arranged between Seleucus and a daughter of Demetrius. This marriage ended, of course, after the birth of a daughter (Stratonice, later married to Antigonus Gonatas) when Seleucus agreed to his wife marrying Antiochus, whether for political reasons (in an attempt to secure Antiochus' position within the 'Macedonian' inner circle) or because Antiochus loved his young stepmother. Shortly after this, Seleucus acted as the middleman between Demetrius and Ptolemy in the arrangement of a marriage between one of Ptolemy's daughters and Demetrius. A marriage between Seleucus and a daughter of Ptolemy was apparently not an option.

Revolts in Asia Minor and Syria immediately followed Seleucus' death, but Antiochus was largely able to crush them; only Bithynia and Cappadocia remained independent. This was a pattern that was to be repeated every

---

2   See Hannestad 2020.

time a king died, and thus each new king had to prove himself through military action.[3] Nonetheless, Bactria was lost to an independent Greco-Bactrian dynasty in about 250, despite a later attempt by Antiochus III to reconquer it. Mesopotamia was lost to the Parthians shortly after the middle of the second century. Part of Syria was at times conquered by the Ptolemies, but later reconquered. In 190, Antiochus III lost Asia Minor after a battle with the Romans. The Seleucids ultimately became kings of Syria and the end came when Syria was conquered by Pompey in 63 BC.

---

3   Austin 2003, 125.

Abbreviations

AIO	*Attic Inscriptions Online*
Basor	*Bulletin of the American Society of Oriental Research*
BCH	*Bulletin de correspondance hellénique*
CRAI	*Comptes rendus de l'Académie des Inscriptions et Belles-Lettres*
JHS	*Journal of Hellenic Studies*
CGRN	*Collection of Greek Ritual Norms (online)*
GRBS	*Greek, Roman and Byzantine Studies*
Ist. Mitt.	*Istanbuler Mitteilungen*
Meditarch	*Mediterranean Archaeology*
OGIS	Dittenberger, W. 1903. *Orientis Graeci Inscriptiones Selectae.* Leipzig.
OJA	*Oxford Journal of Archaeology*
RA	*Revue archéologique*
RAL	*Rendiconti Nazionale dei Lincei, Classe di Scienze morale, storiche e filologiche*
RC	Welles, C. 1934. *Royal Correspondence in the Hellenistic period.* New Haven. Princeton University Press.
SNR	*Schweizeriche numismatische Rundschau*
YBC	*Yale Babylonian Collection*

Bibliography

Abadie-Renaynal, C. and J. Gaborit, 2003. La development urbain de Syrie du Nord: étude dee cas de Séleucie et d'Apamée de l'Euphrate, *Topoi Suppl.* 4, 149–69.

Adams, R. McCormick 1965. *Land behind Baghdad. A History of Settlement on the Diyala Plains.* Chicago and London.

Agostinetti, A.S. 1993. *Flavio Arriano, gli Eventi dopo Alessandro.* Rome.

Alston, R. and O.M. van Nijf (eds.) 2008. *Feeding the ancient Greek City.* Leuven.

Alston, R., O.M. van Nijf and C.G. Williamson 2013. *Cults, Creeds and identities in the Greek City after the Classical Age.* Leuven, Paris, Walpole, MA.

Amandry, M. and O. Callot 1988. Le trésor de Failaka 1984, *Revue Numismatique* 30, 64–74.

Anson, E.M. 2002/2003. The Dating of Perdiccas' Death and the Assembly at Triparadeisus, *Greek, Roman and Byzantine Studies* 43, 373–90.

Anson, E.M. 2004. *Eumenes of Cardia, a Greek among Macedonians.* Leuven.

Antonetti, C. and P. Biagio 2017. *With Alexander in India & Central Asia. Moving East & back to West.* Oxford.

Aphergis, G.G. 2004. *The Seleukid Royal Economy, the Finances and Financial Administration of the Seleukid Empire.* Cambridge.

Aristote *Économique.* 1968. Texte Établi par B.A. Groningen and A. Wartelle. Association Budé Paris.

Armstrong, G.C. 1962. *Aristotle Oeconomica and Magna Moralia.* The Loeb Classical Library. Harvard.

Austin, M.M. 2003. The Seleukids and Asia, in Erskine (ed.) 2003, 212–33.

Austin, M.M. 2006. *The Hellenistic world from Alexander to the Roman conquest. A selection of ancient sources in translation.* Cambridge.

Baker, H.D. The Image of the City in Hellenistic Babylonia, in Stavrianopolou (ed.) 2013, 51–65.

Balty, J.-Ch. 2000. Claudia Apamea. Données nouvelles sur la topographie et l'histoire de l'Apamée, *CRAI* 2000, 459–91.

Balty, J.–Ch.2003. À la recherché de l'Apamée héllenistique: les temoignages archéologiques. *Topoi* Suppl. 4, 223–52.

Baur, P.V.C. 1947. *Dura-Europos* IV, III, *The Lamps.* New Haven.

Baynham, E. 2012 (2010). Arrian's Sources and Reliability, Appendix A, in Romm 2012, 325–32.

Beaulieu, P.-A. 2006. De l'Esagil au Mouseion: l'organisation de la recherché scientifique au IV siècle avant J.-C., in Briant et Joannès 2006, 17–36.

Berlin, A. 2003. Review of Jebel Khalid on the Euphrates: Report on Excavations 1986–1996, Vol. I, *Basor* 331, 88–91.

Bernard, P. 1972. Fouilles d'Aï Khanoum à Aï Khanoum (Afghanistan), *CRAI* 1972, 605–32 (camp. 1971).

Bernard, P. 1973. Fouilles d'Aï Khanoum I (campagnes 1965, 1966, 1967, 1968), rapport préliminaire, *Mémoires de la délégation archéologique française en Afghanistan* 21, 85–102.

Bernard, P. 1976. Campagne de fouilles 1975 à Aï Khanoum (Afghanistan), *CRAI* 1976, 287–322.

Bernard 1978. Campagne de fouilles 1976–77 à Aï Khanoum (Afghanistan), *CRAI* 1978, 429–41.

Bernard P. 2008. The Greek Colony at Ai Khanoum and Hellenism in Central Asia, in Hiebert and Cambon (eds.), 44–55.

Bernard, V., J. Gachet and J.-F. Salles 1990. Apostilles en marge de la céramique des États IV and V de la forteresse, *FFF* 1986–1988. Failaka. Fouilles Françaises. Paris.

Bilde, P., T. Engberg-Pedersen, L. Hannestad, (eds.) 1992. *Centre and Periphery in the Hellenistic World* (Studies in Hellenistic Civilization 4). Aarhus.

Billows, Richard A. *Kings and Colonists: Aspects of Macedonian Imperialism*. 1995. Brill.

Billows, Richard A. 1997. *Antigonos the One-Eyed and the Creation of the Hellenistic State*. Berkeley.

Boehmer, R.M., F. Pedde and B. Salle 1995. *Uruk. Die Gräber. Ausgrabungen in Uruk-Warka* (Endberichte 10). Mainz.

Boiy, T. 2000. Dating methods during the early Hellenistic period, *Journal of Cuneiform Studies* 52, 115–20.

Boiy, T. 2004. Late Achaemenid and Hellenistic Babylon. *Orientalia Lovaniensia Analecta* 136,116–7.

Boiy, T. 2007. *Between High and Low. A chronology of the early Hellenistic period*. Frankfurt am Main.

Boiy, T. 2010. Royal and Satrapal Armies in Babylonia during the Second Diadoch War. The *Chronicle of the Successors* on the Events during the Seventh Year of Philip Arrhidaeus (=317/316 BC), *JHS* 130, 1–13.

Boiy, T. 2011. The Reigns of the Seleucid Kings According to the Babylonian King List, *Journal of Near Eastern Studies* 70, 1–12.

Boiy, T. 2013. The Diadochi History in Cuneiform Documentation, in Troncoso and Anson (eds.) 2013, 7–16.

Bosworth, A.B. 1988. *From Arrian to Alexander*. Oxford.

Bosworth, A.B. 2002. *The Legacy of Alexander: Politics, Warfare, and Propaganda under the Successors*. Oxford.

Bosworth, A.B. 2012 (2010). Alexander's Death: The Poisoning Rumors. Appendix P, in Romm (ed.) 2012, 407–10.

Boucharlat, R. 1993. Pottery in Susa during the Seleucid, Parthian and early Sasanian periods, in Finkbeiner (ed.) 1993, 41–58.

Briant, P. 2002. *From Cyrus to Alexander: A History of the Persian Empire*. Winona Lake.

Briant, P. et F. Joannès 2006. *La transition entre l'empire achéménide et les royaumes hellénistiques (vers 350–300 av. J.-C.)*. Paris.

Buraselis, K. 1982. *Das hellenistische Makedonien und die Ägäis*. Munich.

Burgh, Glenn R. (ed.) 2006. *The Cambridge Companion to the Hellenistic World*. Cambridge.

Campbell, B. and L.A. Tritle (eds.) 2013. *The Oxford Handbook of Warfare in the Classical World*. Oxford.

Capdetrey, L. 2007. *Le pouvoir séleucide. Territoire, administration, finances d'un royaume hellénistique (312–129 avant J.-C.)*. Rennes.

Cartledge, P., P. Garnsey and E. Gruen (eds.) 1997. *Hellenistic Constructs: Essay in Culture, History and Historiography*. Berkeley, Los Angeles, London.

Cartledge, P. 2012. Introduction, in Romm (ed.) and Mensch (translation) 2012, pp. XIII–XXVIII.

Canali di Rossi, F. 2004. *Inschriften griechischer Städte aus Kleinasien 65: Iscrizioni dello estremo oriente greco*. Bonn.

Chaniotis, A. 2005. *War in the Hellenistic World*. Oxford.

Clairmont, C. 1956–7. Greek Pottery in the Near-East II. Black Vases, *Berytus* XII,1, 1 ff.

Clarke, G.W. 2002. *The Governor's Palace, Jebel Khalid* vol. 1 (Meditarch Supplement 5). Sydney, 25–48.

Clarke, G.W. 2005. Jebel Khalid: Area B: The Jebel Khalid Temple, *Meditarch* 18, 128–35.

Clarke, G.W. 2006. The Jebel Khalid Temple, *Meditarch* 19/20. 133–9.

Clarke, G.W. 2008. Area B, the Jebel Khalid Temple, *Meditarch* 21, 59–78.

Clarke, G.W. 2009. Area B, the Temple precinct, *Meditarch* 22/23, 207–8.

Cohen, G.M. 1995. *The Hellenistic Settlements in Europe, the Islands, and Asia Minor*. Berkeley.

Cohen, G.M. 2013. *The Hellenistic Settlements in the East from Armenia and Mesopotamia to Bactria and India*. Berkeley.

Comfort, M., C. Abadie-Renal and R. Ergec 2000. Crossing the Euphrates in Antiquity: Zeugma seen from Space, *Anatolian Studies* 50, 99–126.

Connelly, J. 1990. *Fouilles Françaises de Failaka 1986–1988*. The Terracotta Figurines – Greek Types and Influences. Paris, 209–18.

Connor, P. and G. Clarke. 2002. The Northwest Tower and the Main Gate *Jebel Khalid* vol. 1 (Meditarch Supplement 5). Sydney, 1–30.

Coulton, J.J. 1977. *The Architectural Development of the Greek Stoa*. Oxford.

Caubet, A. and J.-F. Salles 1984. *Fouilles Françaises de Failaka*. Le sanctuaire Hellénistique B6, 73–156. Paris.

Curtis, J. & N. Tallis 2005. *Forgotten Empire. The World of Ancient Persia*. Berkeley, Los Angeles.

Damsgaard-Madsen, A., E. Christiansen and E. Hallager 1988. *Studies in Ancient History and Numismatics*. Aarhus.

De Giordi, A.U. 2016. *Ancient Antioch from the Seleucid Era to the Islamic Conquest*. Cambridge.

Del Monte, G. 1997. *Testa dalla Babilonia ellenistica*. Pisa.

Derks, T. and N. Roymans (eds.) 2009. *Ethnic Constructs in antiquity: the role of power and tradition*. Amsterdam.

Desmenaux, A., J. Gaborit and J.-S. Caillou 1999. Nouvelles découvertes à Apamée d'Osrhoene. *CRAI* 1999, 78–105.

Deubner, O. 1957. Die griechische Scherben von Babylon, in Wetzel, Schmidt and Mallwitz (eds.) 1957, 51–8.

Dmitriev, S. 2007. The Last Marriage and the death of Lysimachus, *GRBS* 47, 135–49.

Doty, L.T. 1988. Nikarchos and Kephalon, in Leichty et al. (eds.) 1988, 95–118.

Dyggve, E., F. Poulsen and K. Rhomaios 1934. *Das Heroon von Kalydon*. Copenhagen.

Engels, D.W. 1978. *Alexander the Great and the Logistics of the Macedonia Army*. Berkeley.

Errington, R.M. 1970. From Babylon to Triparadeisos: 323–320 B.C., *JHS* 90, 49–77.

Errington, R.M. 1977. Diodorus Siculus and the Chronology of the Early Diadochi, 320–311 B.C. *Hermes* 105, 478–504.

Errington, R.M. 2008. *A History of the Hellenistic World*. Hoboken.

Erskine, A. (ed.). 2003. *A Companion to the Hellenistic World*. Malden and Oxford.

Falkenstein. A. 1941. *Topographie von Uruk. Uruk zur Seleukidenzeit*. Leipzig.

Finkbeiner, U. 1993. *Materialien zur Archäologie der Seleukiden- und Partherzeit im südlichen Babylonien und Golfgebiet*. Tübingen.

Fleischer, R. 1991. *Studien zur seleukidischen Kunst*. Mainz.

Foldvari, P. and B. van Leeuwen 2015. Market performance in early economies: concepts and empirics, with an application to Babylon, in Spek, van der Leeuwen and van Zanden (eds.) 2015, 19–44.

Francfort, H.-P. 1984. *Fouilles d'Äi Khanoum* III. *Le sanctuaire du temple à niches indentées 2. Les Trouvailles*, (Mémoires de la Délégation Archéologique Française en Afghanistan 27). Paris.

Franke, U. and J. Gierlichs (eds.) 2011. *Roads of Arabia: Archaeological Treasures from Saudi Arabia*. Berlin and Tübingen.

Fraser, D. 1991. Alanbrooke, in Keegan (ed.) 1991, 89–103.

Frézouls, E. (ed.) 1987. *Sociétés urbaines, sociétés rurales dans l'Asie Mineure et la Syrie hellénistiques et romains*. Céramique et peuplement du chalcolithique à la conquête arabe. Paris.

Gardin, J.-C. 1998. *Prospections Archéologiques en Bactriane Orientale (1974–1978)* vol. 3. *Description des sites et notes de synthèse*. Paris.

Geer, R.M. 1954. *Diodorus Siculus XVIII–XIX*, 65. Loeb edition.

Geller, G.J. and H. Maehler in collaboration with A.D.E. Lewis. 1995. *Legal Documents of the Hellenistic World*, London.

Graf, D.E. 1994. The Persian Royal Road System, in Sancisi-Weerden, Kuhrt and Cool Root (eds.), 167–89.

Grainger, J.D. 1990. *Seleukos Nikator, Building a Hellenistic Kingdom*. London.

Grainger, J.D. 2014. *The Rise of the Seleucid Empire 323–223 BC*. Barnsley.

Grayson, A.K. 1975. *Babylonian Historical-Literary Texts*. Toronto and Buffalo.

Günther. W. 1971. *Das Orakel von Didyma in hellenistischer Zeit. Eine Interpretation von Stein-Urkunden* (4. Beiheft Ist. Mitt). Tübingen.

Hadley, R.J. 1974. Seleucus, Dionysus, or Alexander, *Numismatic Chronicle* 14, 9–13.

Hammond, N.G.L. and F.W. Walbank 1988. *A History of Macedonia* Vol. III, 336–167 B.C. Oxford.

Hannestad, L. 1983. *Ikaros: The Hellenistic Settlements*, vols. 2,1 and 2,2. *The Hellenistic Pottery from Failaka, with a survey of Hellenistic Pottery in the Near East*. Aarhus.

Hannestad, L. 2013a. A comparative study of the cultural dynamics of two cities in the eastern Seleukid empire: Uruk and Ai Khanoum, in Lindström, Hansen, Wieczorek and Tellenbach 2013, 99–113.

Hannestad, L. 2013b. A Royal Signature Landscape: New Light on the Transformation of Northern Syria after the Conquest of Alexander, in Ivanchik (ed.) 2013, 250–274. Moscow.

Hannestad, L. 2019. On the Periphery of the Seleucid Empire: Failaka revisited, in
Oetjen, R. (ed.) 2019, 312-332. Berlin.

Hannestad, L. 2020. The Macedonian. Seleukos I – the foreign king. In press.

Hannestad, L. and D. Potts 1990. Temple Architecture in the Seleucid Kingdom, in
Bilde, Engberg-Petersen, Hannestad and Zahle (eds.) 1990, 91–124.

Heckel, W. 1992. *The Marshals of Alexander's Empire*. London. Abingdon.

Heckel, W. 2006. *Who is Who in the Age of Alexander the Great*. Oxford.

Heckel, W. 2013. The Three Thousand: Alexander's Infantry Guard, in Campbell and
Tritle 2013, 162–78.

Heckel, W. and L.A. Tritle (eds.). 2009. *Alexander the Great A New History*. London.

Hiebert, F. and P. Cambon (eds.) 2008. *Afghanistan. Hidden Treasures from the National
Museum, Kabul*. Washington.

Hoffmann, A., R. Posamentir and M. Sayar (eds.) 2011. *Hellenismus in der Kilikia Pedia*
(Byzas 14). Istanbul

Hoover, O.D. 2002. The identity of the helmeted head on the "victory" coinage of Susa,
SNR 81, 51–64.

Hopkins, C. 1979. The Discovery of Dura-Europos. New Haven.

Hornblower, J. 1981. *Hieronymus of Cardia*. Oxford.

Houghton, A. and C. Lorber 2002. *Seleucid Coins: A Comprehensive Catalogue*. Part 1:
Seleucus through Antiochus III. American Numismatic Society. New York.

Howland, D. 1958. *Greek Lamps and their Survival. The Athenian Agora* Vol. 4. Princeton.

Hughes, J. Donald 2013. Warfare and Environments in the Ancient World, in Campbell
and Tritle (eds.) 2013, 128–39.

Huijs, J.A.M., R. Pirngruber and B. van Leeuwen 2015. Climate, War and Economic
Development: the case of second-century BC Babylon, in Spek, van der Leeuwen
and van Zanden (eds.) 2015, 128–48.

Huth, M. and P. van Alfen 2010. Coinage of Caravan Kingdoms: Studies in the Monetiza-
tion of Ancient Arabia, *Numismatic Studies* 25, 65–82.

Hübner, G. 1993. *Die Applikenkeramik von Pergamon. Eine Bildsprache im Dienst des
Herrscherkultes*. Berlin/New York.

Højrup, O. 1982. *Herregårdsliv, beretninger fra århundredeskiftet. Herskabet*. Copenhagen.

Invernizzi, A. 1976. Ten Years' Research in the Al-Mada'in Area, Seleucia and Ctesiphon,
Sumer 32, 167–75.

Invernizzi, A. 1990. Arte seleucide in Mesopotamia, *Akten des 13. Internationalen Kon-
gresses für klassische Archäologie* (Berlin 1988). Mainz.

Invernizzi, A. 1992. Seleucia on the Tigris. Centre and periphery in Seleucid Asia, in
Bilde, Engberg-Pedersen and Hannestad (eds.) 1992, 230–50.

Invernizzi, A. 1994. Babylonian Motifs on the Sealings from Seleucia-on-the-Tigris, in
Sancisi-Weerdenburg and Kuhrt (eds.) 1994, 353–64.

Invernizzi, A. 1998. Portraits of Seleucid Kings on the sealings from Seleucia-on-the-Tigris: a Reassessment, *Bulletin of the Asia Institute New Series* 12, *Alexander's Legacy
in the East, Studies in Honor of Paul Bernard*, 105–12.

Invernizzi, A. 2004. *Seleucia al Tigri. Le impronte di sigillo dagli Archive* I–III. Alessan-
dria.

Iossip, P. 2012. Les "cornes" des Seleucides: vers une divinisation "discrète" , *Cahiers des
études anciennes* XLIX, 43–147.

Isager, S. 1988. Once upon a Time, in A. Damsgaard-Madsen, E. Christiansen and E.
Hallager (eds.) 1988, 77–83.

Ivanchik, A.I. (ed.) 2013. *Monumentum Gregorianum. Sbornik naucnych statej pamjati akademika Grigorija Maksimivocha Bongard-Levin.* Moscow.

Jackson, H. 2006. *Jebel Khalid* vol. 2. *The terracotta Figurines* (Meditarch supplement 6). Sydney.

Jackson, H. 2014. *Jebel Khalid* vol. 4. *The Housing Insula* (Meditarch supplement 9). Sydney.

Jackson, H. and J. Tidmarsh 2011. *Jebel Khalid on the Euphrates* vol. 3, *The Pottery.* Meditarch Supplement 7. Sydney.

Jeppesen, K. 1960. Et kongeligt sendebud til Ikaros (with English summary), *KUML* 10, 153–98.

Jeppesen, K. 1989. *Ikaros, the Hellenistic Settlements* vol. 3: *The Sacred Enclosure in the Early Hellenistic Period.* Aarhus.

Karvonen-Kannas, K. 1995. *The Seleucid and Parthian Terracotta Figurines from Babylon.* Firenze.

Keegan, J. (ed.) 1991. *Churchill's Generals.* London.

Koldewey, R. 1914. *The Excavations of Babylon.* London.

Kose, A. and H.-G. Bartel 1998. *Uruk: Architektur IV: von der Seleukiden bis zur Sassanidenzeit.* Mainz.

Kosmin. P.J. 2014. *The Land of the Elephant Kings. Space, Territory and Ideology in the Seleucid Empire.* Cambridge Mass.

Kosmin, P.J. 2018. *Time and its Adversaries in the Seleucid Empire.* Cambridge, Mass. and London.

Kramer, N. 2004. *Gindaros: Geschichte und Archäologie einer Siedlung im nordwestlichen Syrien von hellenistischer bis in frühbyzantinischer Zeit.* Rahden/Westf.

Krentz, P. and E.L. Wheeler 1994. *Polyaenus Stratagems of War* Vols. 1–2. Chicago (also online by Cambridge University Press 2009).

Kritt, B. 1996. *Seleucid Coins of Bactria* (Classical Numismatic Studies no. 1). Lancaster/London.

Kritt, B. 1997. *The Early Seleucid Mint of Susa* (Classical Numismatic Studies no. 2), 80–107.

Kuhrt, A. and S. Sherwin-White 1987. *Hellenism in the East The Interaction of Greek and Non-Greek Civilizations from Syria to Central-Asia.* London..

Langin-Hooper, S. 2007. Social networks and Cross-cultural Interaction: A new Interpretation of the Female Terracotta Figurines of Hellenistic Babylon, *OJA* 26(2), 145–65.

Lecuyot, G. 2013. *Fouilles d'Ai Khanoum* Vol. IX. *L'habitat.* Paris.

Leichty, E. et al. (eds.) 1988. *A Scientific Humanist: Studies in Memory of Abraham Sachs.* Philadelphia.

Leriche, P. 1987. Urbanisme défensif et occupation de territoire en Syrie hellénistique, in Frézouls (ed.) 1987, 57–79.

Leriche, P. 2003. Doura Europos héllenistique: les témoignages archéologiques, *Topoi Suppl.* 4, 171–91.

Leriche, P. 2004. La rue principale et l'urbanisme d'Europos-Doura, étude préliminaire, *Parthica* 6, 145–59.

Leriche, P. 2007. *La città dell'Oriente ellenistico, Sulla via di Alessandro da Seleucia al Gandhara,* Milano, 83–91.

Leriche, P. and M. Gelin 1997. Le palais du stratège, *Doura-Europos Ètudes IV*. 1991–
1993. Beirut, 55–80.

Lerner, J. 2003–4. Correcting the Early History of Ay Kanom, *Archäologische Mitteilungen aus Iran und Turan* 35–6, 373–410.

Lindström. G. 2003. *Uruk: Siegelabdrücke aud hellenistischen Tonbullen und Tontafeln*.
Mainz.

Lindström, G., S. Hansen, A. Wieczorek and M. Tellenbach. 2013. *Zwischen Ost und
West – neue Forschungen zum antiken Zentralasien*. Berlin.

Lorber, C. 2005. A revised chronology for the coinage of Ptolemy I, *Numismatic Chronicle* 165, 45–64.

Lyonnet, B. 2012. Questions on the Date of the Hellenistic Pottery from Central Asia (Ai
Khanoum, Marakanda and Koktepe), *Ancient Civilizations from Scythia to Siberia*
vol. 18, 143–73.

Ma, J. 2003. Kings, in Erskine (ed.) 2003, 177–95.

Mairs, R. 2013. The 'Temple with Indented Niches' at Ai Khanoum. Ethnic and Civic
Identity in Hellenistic Bactria, in Alston, van Nijf and Williamson (eds.) 2013,
85–117.

Malay, H. and M. Ricl 2009. Two new Hellenistic Decrees from Aigai in Aiolis, *Epigraph-
ica Anatolica* 42, 39–60.

Mallwitz, A. 1957. Das Theater von Babylon, in Wetzel, Schmidt and Mallwitz (eds.)
1957, 3–22.

Manni, E. 1949. Tre noti di cronologia ellenistica, *RAL* 8, 53–85.

Martinez-Sève, L. 2002a. *Les figurines de Suse de l'époque néo-élamite à l'époque sassa-
nide*. Paris.

Martinez-Séve, L. 2002b. La ville de Suse à l'époque hellénistique, *RA* 2002, 31–53.

Martinez-Sève, L. 2014. The Spatial Organization of Ai Khanoum, a Greek City in
Afghanistan, *AJA* 118, 267–83.

Martinez-Sève, L. 2015. Ai Khanoum and Greek Domination in Central Asia, *Electrum*
22, 17–46.

Mathiesen, H.E. 1982. *Ikaros, the Hellenistic Settlements* vol. 1. *The Terracottas*. Aarhus.

McDowell, R.H. 1935. *Stamped and inscribed objects from Seleucia on the Tigris*. Ann
Arbor.

Meadows, A. R. 2005. The Administration of the Achaemenid Empire, in Curtis and
Tallis (eds.) 2005, 181–209.

Meeus, A. 2012. Diodoros and the chronology of the third Diadoch War, *Phoenix* 66,
74–66.

Mehl, A. 1986. *Seleukos Nikator und sein Reich*. Leuven.

Menegazzi, R. 2014. *Seleucia al Tigri. Terracotte dagli scavi italiani e americani* I–III.
Florence.

Messina, V. 2011. Seleucia on the Tigris. The Babylonian Polis of Antiochus I, *Mesopotamia, Rivista di archeologia* Vol. 46, 157–67.

Messina, V. 2017. Aspects of Seleucid Iconography and Kingship, in Antonetti and Biagio
(eds.) 2017, 17–36.

Miller, R.P. and K.R. Walters 2004. Seleucid coinage and the legend of the horned
Bucephalas, *Schweizerische numismatische Rundschau* 83, 44–54.

Mørkholm, O. 1991. *Early Hellenistic Coinage*. Cambridge.

Nixon, C.E.V. 2002. The Coins, in *Jebel Khalid* vol. 1 (Meditarch Supplement 5), 291–335.

Oetjen. R. (ed.) 2020. *New Perspectives in Seleucid History, Archaeology and Numismatics. Studies in Honor of Getzel M. Cohen.* Berlin.
Ogden, D. 2017. *The Legend of Seleucus.* Cambridge.

Potts, D.T. 2010. The Circulation of Foreign Coins within Arabia and Arabian Coins outside the Peninsula in the Pre-Islamic Era, in Huth and van Alfen (eds.) 2010, 65–82.
Potts, D.T. 2016. *The Archaeology of Elam. Formation and Transformation of an Ancient Iranian State.* New York.
Potts, D.T. 2018. The Carian Villages, *Cuneiform Digital Library Bulletin* 2018:2, 1–7.

Radt, T. 2011. Die Ruinen auf dem Karasis. Eine befestigte hellenistiche Reidenz in Taurus, in Hoffmann, Posamentir and Sayar (eds.) 2011, 37–62.
Rapin, C. 1983. Les inscriptions économiques de la trésorie d'Ai Khanoum, *BCH* 107, 315–72.
Rapin, C. 1992. *Fouilles d'ÄiKhanoum VIII. La trésorie du palais héllenistique d'Äikhanoum. L'apogée et la chute du royaume grec de Bactriane.* Paris.
Reuther, O. 1968. *Die Innenstadt von Babylon (Merkes).* Osnabrück (reprint from 1926).
Robert, L. 1968. De Delphes à l'Oxus. Inscriptions grecques nouvelles de la Bactriane, *CRAI* 112, 416–7.
Roisman, J. (ed.) 2003. *Brill's Companion to Alexander the Great.* Leiden.
Roisman, J. 2012. *Alexander's Veterans and the Early Wars of the Successors.* Austin.
Roller, D.W. 2016. Megasthenes: his life and work, in Wiesehöfer, Brinkhaus and Bichler 2016, 119–27.
Romm, James. 2011. *Ghost on the Throne: The Death of Alexander the Great and the War for Crown and Empire.* New York.
Romm, J. (ed.) and P. Mensch (translation) 2012. *The Landmark Arrian. The Campaigns of Alexander. Anabasis Alexandrou.* New York.
Romm, J. 2012. Appendix D, in Romm and Mensch 2012, 343–51.
Rostovtzeff, M. 1941. *The Social and Economic History of the Hellenistic World.* Oxford.
Rotroff, S.I. 1982. *Hellenistic Pottery. Athenian and Imported Moldmade Bowls* (The Athenian Agora vol. 22). Princeton.
Rotroff, S.I. 1997. *Hellenistic Pottery Athenian and Imported Wheelmade Table Ware and Related Ware* (The Athenian Agora vol. 24). Princeton.
Rouché, Ch. and S. Sherwin-White 1985. Some Aspects of the Seleucid Empire: the Greek inscriptions from Failaka in the Arabian Gulf, *Chiron* 1985, 1- 35
Rougement, G. 2012. *Inscriptions grecques d'Iran et d'Asie central.* (Corpus Inscriptionum Iranicarum II/I). London.

Sachs, A. J. and H. Hunger 1988. *Astronomical Diaries and Related Texts from Babylonia* Vol. 1 from 652 to 262. Vienna. Verlag der Östereichischen Akademie.
Sachs, A. and J. Wiseman. 1954. A Babylonian King List of the Hellenistic Period, *Iraq* 16,2, 202–11.
Salles, J.F. 1988. The Arab-Persian Gulf under the Seleucids, Kuhrt and Sherwin-White, 75–109.
Savalli-Lestrade, I. 1998 l. *Les philoi royaux dans'Asie hellénistique.* Geneva.

Sancisi-Weerdenburg, H., A. Kuhrt and M. Cool Root (eds.) 1994. *Achaemenid History VIII, Continuity and Change*. Leiden.

Sauvaget, J. 1934. Le plan de Laodicée-sur-mer, *Bulletin d'Études Orientales* 4, 81–114.

Sauvaget, J. 1936. Le plan de Laodicée-sur-mer (note complémentaire), *Bulletin d'Études Orientales* 6, 51–2.

Scheidel,W., I. Morris and R.P. Saller (eds.) 2007. *The Cambridge economy history of the Greco-Roman world*. Cambridge.

Schlumberger, D. 1969. Triparadeisos, *Bulletin du Musée de Beyrouth* 22, 147–49.

Schober, L. 1981. *Untersuchungen zur Geschichte Babyloniens und der Oberen Satrapien von 323–303 v. Chr*. Frankfurt.

Sherwin-White, S. 1982. A Greek Ostrakon from Babylonof the Early third Century B.C., *Zeitschrift für Papyrologie und Epigraphic* 47, 51–70.

Sherwin-White, S. and A. Kuhrt. 1993. *From Samarkand to Sardis. A New Approach to the Seleucid Empire*. Berkeley and Los Angeles.

Slotsky A.L. 1997. *The Bourse of Babylon: an analysis of the market quotations in the Astronomical Diaries of Babylonia*. Bethesda, Md.

Soldt, W.H. (ed.) 2001. *Studies presented to Klaas R. Veenhof on the occasion of his sixty fifth birthday*. Leiden.

Spek, R.J. van der 1985. The Babylonian temple under Macedonian and Parthian domination, *Bibliotheca Orientalis* 42, 541–62.

Spek, R.J. van der 1993. *Bibliotheca Orientalis* L. No. 1/2, 91–101.

Spek, R.J. van der 1995. Land Ownership in Babylonian Cuneiform Documents, in Geller and Maehler (eds.) 1995, 173–245.

Spek, R.J. van der 2001. Ethnic Segregation in Hellenistic Babylon, in Soldt (ed.) 2001, 445–56.

Spek, Robert van der 2007. The Hellenistic Near East, in Scheidel, Morris and Saller (eds.), chapter 5.

Spek, R.J. van der 2008. Feeding Hellenistic Seleucia on the Tigris and Babylon, in Alston and van Nijf (eds.) 2008, 33–45.

Spek, R.J. van der 2009. Multi-ethnicity and ethnic segregation in Hellenistic Babylon, in Derks and Roymans (eds.) 2009, 101–115.

Spek, R.J. van der, B. van Leeuwen and J.L. van Zanden 2015. *A History of Market Performance*. Abingdon.

Spek R.J. van der, B. van der Leeuwen, J. Luiten van Zanden (eds.) 2015. *A History of Market Performance. From ancient Babylonia to the modern world*. Abingdon and New York.

Stavrianopolou, E. (ed.) 2013. *Shifting Social Imaginaries in the Hellenistic Period*. Leiden.

Stevens, K. 2014. The Antiochus Cylinder, Babylonian Scholarship and Seleucid Imperial Ideology, *JHS* 134, 66–88.

Stewart. A. 1993. *Faces of Power: Alexander's Image and Hellenistic Politics*. Oakland.

Stillwell, R. 1941. *Antioch-on-the-Orontes* III. Princeton.

Strommenger, E. 1967. *Gefässe aus Uruk von der neubabylonischen Zeit bis zu den Sassaniden* (Ausgrabungen der deutschen Forschungsgemeinschaftin Uruk-Warka 7). Berlin.

Strootman, R. 2011. Kings and Cities of the Hellenistic Age, in Alston, van Nijf and Williamson (ed.) 2011, 141–53.

Strootman, R. 2013. Babylonian, Macedonian, King of the World: The Antiochos Cylinder from Borsippa and Seleukid Integration, in Stavrianopoulou (ed.) 2013, 67–98.

Strootman, R. 2014. *Courts and Elites in the Hellenistic Empires. The Near East after the Achaemenids, c. 330 to 30 BCE.* Edinburgh.

Temin, P. 2002. Price Behaviour in Ancient Babylonia, *Explorations in Economic History* 39, 46–60.

Temin, P. 2001. Price Behaviour in Ancient Babylonia. https://economics.mit.edu/files/7258

Thompson, D. 1997. The Infrastructure of Splendour: Census and Taxes in Ptolemaic Egypt, in Cartledge, Garnsey and Gruen (eds.) 1997, 242–57.

Thompson, D.J. 2006. The Hellenistic Family, in Burgh (ed.) 2006, 93–112.

Thonemann. P. 2015. *The Hellenistic World. Using Coins as Sources.* Cambridge.

Troncoso, V.A. and E.M. Anson 2013. *After Alexander. The Time of the Diadochi (323–281 BC).* Oxford and Oakville.

Trundle, M. 2004. *Greek Mercenaries. From the Late Archaic Period to Alexander.* London and New York.

Tuchelt, K. 1973. *Vorarbeiten zu einer Topographie von Didyma (Istanbuler Mitteilungen Beiheft 9).* Tübingen.

van Groningen, B.A. and A. Wartelle. 1968. Aristote, Économique (Collection Budé). Paris.

van Ingen, W. 1939. *Figurines from Seleucia on the Tigris.* Ann Arbor.

Veuve, S. 1987. *Fouilles d'Aï Khanoum VI. Le Gymnase. Architecture, céramique, sculpture. Mémoires de la delegation archéologique française en Afghanistan 30.* Paris.

Waerzeggers, C. 2012. The Babylonian Chronicles: Classification and Provenance, *JNS* 71, 285–98.

Walbank, F.W. 1988. In Hammond and Walbank (eds.) 1988. 199–364.

Walton, F.R. 1957. Diodorus Siculus Books XXI–XXXII. Loeb edition. London.

Waterfield, R. 2011. *Dividing the Spoils. The War for Alexander the Great's Empire.* Oxford.

Wetzel, F., E. Schmidt and A. Mallwitz 1957. *Das Babylon der Spätzeit.* Berlin.

Wheatly, P. 1998. The Chronology of the Third Diadoch War, *Phoenix* 52, 257–81.

Wheatly, P. 2002. Antigonus Monophthalmus in Babylonia 310–308 B.C., *Journal of Near Eastern Studies* 2002, 39–47

Wheatley, P. 2009. The Diadochi, or Successors of Alexander, in Heckel and Tritle (eds.) 2009, 53–68.

Wiesehöfer, J, H. Brinkhaus and R. Bichler, (eds.) 2016. *Megastenes und seine Zeit.* Wiesbaden. Wilkinson, T.J. 2003. *Archaeological landscapes of the Near East.* Tucson.

Yon. J.-B. 2003. Les villes de Haute-Mésopotamie et de l'Euphrate, *Topoi Suppl.* 4, 193–210.

Yonge, C.D. (translator) 1854. *The Deipnosophists; or Banquet of the Learned, of Athenaeus.* London.

Ziegler, Ch. 1962. *Die Terrakotten von Warka* (Ausgrabungen der deutschen Forschungsgemeinschaft in Uruk-Warka Band 6). Berlin.

Index

Photo credits

Fig. 1   Jhelum/Hydaspes River. Wikipedia.
Fig. 2   The tomb of Cyrus. Photo: Isa Pakdel.
Fig. 3   The Istanbul Archaeological Museum. Photo: Getty Images.
Fig. 4   British Museum, London.
Fig. 5   Münzcabinett Berlin.
Fig. 6   Museum of the Royal Tombs Vergina
Fig. 7   Wikipedia, photo: Zeynel Cebeci.
Fig. 8   New Carlsberg Glyptotek, Copenhagen.
Fig. 9.   British Museum, London.
Fig. 10   Münzcabinett Berlin.
Fig. 11   After Invernizzi 2004, Pl. 13, SU 6: S74682.
Fig. 12   Münzcabinett Berlin.
Fig. 13   Photo: Heritage Auctions.
Fig. 14   Münzcabinett Berlin.
Fig. 15   Photo: Alamy.
Fig. 16   After Messina, V 2011.
Fig. 17   After Hannestad 2013a, p. 106, fig. 14.
Fig. 18   After Hannestad 2013b, p. 261, fig. 3.
Fig. 19   Photo: Hanna Lei Camp.
Fig. 20   After Hannestad 2013a, p. 101, fig. 4.
Fig. 21   After Hannestad 2013a, p. 102, fig. 5.
Fig. 22   After Hannestad 2013a, p. 103, fig. 11.
Fig. 23   After Menegazzi 2014 Tav. A no.3 G186.
Fig. 24   After Fra Karvonen-Kannas K. Pl. 10 nos. 50-51.
Fig. 25   After Hannestad 2013a, p. 103, fig. 8.
Fig. 26   After Hannestad 2013a, p. 102, fig. 6.
Fig. 27   After Invernizzi 2004, pl. 4 alk 36 (B9: S7-7972).
Fig. 28   After Invernizzi 2004, frontcover.
Fig. 29   Photo: Kristian Jeppesen.
Fig. 30   After Hannestad 2013a, p. 108, fig. 17.
Fig. 31   After Hannestad 2013a, p. 107, fig. 15.
Fig. 32   Bridgeman Art Library/Scanpix.
Fig. 33   Photo: Délégation Archéologique Française en Afghanistan, DAFA.
Fig. 34   After Clarke 2002.
Fig. 35   After Clarke 2006.
Fig. 36   Sherwin-White 1982.

The Hellenistic World

Tanais (Don)

Sea of Azov

Danube

Black Sea

MACEDONIA

THRACE   Byzantium   PONTUS

Pella   Lysimachaia   Heraclea
                          Pontica
Aigai   SAMOTRACE   Cyzicus
EPIRUS   THESSALY   LEMNOS   TROAS   Doryleion   ARMENIA
                          Pergamum
AITOLIA   LESBOS   Ephesus
ACHAIA   Sardis   PHRYGIA   CAPPADOCIA
Athens   Magnesia   CARIA   Zeugma   Gaugamela
Corinth   Didyma   Tarsus   Issus   Jebel Khalid
          COS   LYCIA   PAMPHYLIA   Seleucia   Antioch   MESOPOTAMIA
          RHODES   Laodicaea   SYRIA   Apamea
          CRETE   CYPRUS   Dura-
                          Europus   Euphrates
Mediterranean Sea   PHOENICIA   Babylo
                    Sidon   Damascus
                    Tyre
Cyrene   KOILE SYRIA
                    Gaza   Jerusalem
          Alexandria   Pelusium
          Memphis
          EGYPT   ARABIA
                    Nile
          Thebes   Red Sea